Cambridge Elements ≡

Elements in Historical Theory and Practice
edited by
Daniel Woolf
Queen's University, Ontario

THE FABRIC
OF HISTORICAL TIME

Zoltán Boldizsár Simon
Bielefeld University

Marek Tamm
Tallinn University

Shaftesbury Road, Cambridge CB2 8EA, United Kingdom

One Liberty Plaza, 20th Floor, New York, NY 10006, USA

477 Williamstown Road, Port Melbourne, VIC 3207, Australia

314–321, 3rd Floor, Plot 3, Splendor Forum, Jasola District Centre, New Delhi – 110025, India

103 Penang Road, #05–06/07, Visioncrest Commercial, Singapore 238467

Cambridge University Press is part of Cambridge University Press & Assessment, a department of the University of Cambridge.

We share the University's mission to contribute to society through the pursuit of education, learning and research at the highest international levels of excellence.

www.cambridge.org
Information on this title: www.cambridge.org/9781009108331

DOI: 10.1017/9781009103947

First published 2023

A catalogue record for this publication is available from the British Library

ISBN 978-1-009-10833-1 Paperback
ISSN 2634-8616 (online)
ISSN 2634-8608 (print)

The Fabric of Historical Time

Elements in Historical Theory and Practice

DOI: 10.1017/9781009103947
First published online: July 2023

Zoltán Boldizsár Simon
Bielefeld University

Marek Tamm
Tallinn University

Author for correspondence: Zoltán Boldizsár Simon, zoltanbsimon@uni-bielefeld.de

Abstract: Historical time is a notoriously elusive notion. Yet, as societies attempt to make sense of rapidly changing worlds, it gains a new significance in the twenty-first century. This Element sketches a theory of historical time as based on a distinction between temporality and historicity. It approaches the fabric of historical time as varying relational arrangements and interactions of multiple temporalities and historicities. In the fabric, kinds of temporalities and historicities emerge, come to being, fade out, transform, cease to exist, merge, coexist, overlap, arrange and rearrange in constellations, and clash and conflict in a dynamic without a predetermined plot. The Element pays special attention to the more-than-human temporalities of the Anthropocene, the technology-fueled historicities of runaway changes, and the conflicts in the fabric of historical time at the intersections of technological, ecological, and social change.

Keywords: historical time, multiple historicities, multiple temporalities, synchronization, time conflicts

ISBNs: 9781009108331 (PB), 9781009103947 (OC)
ISSNs: 2634-8616 (online), 2634-8608 (print)

Contents

Introduction: The Fabric of Historical Time   1

1 Modern Historical Time and Its Exhaustion   9

2 A New Multiplicity of Historical Times   19
   Figures of Historical Time   24
   Multiple Temporalities   32
   Multiple Historicities   40

3 Conflicts in the Fabric of Historical Time   45
   Time Conflicts in Synchronized Time   46
   Conflicts of Desynchronized Temporalities
   and Historicities   48

One Fabric, Many Times: A Resolution   53

References   56

Introduction: The Fabric of Historical Time

At the turn of the millennium, theoretical physicists seemed keen to explore the fabric of the universe. Although attempting to unravel the workings of the universe is not an endeavor specific to that moment, there was something new to these efforts: the "fabric" metaphor, which came to dominate such attempts. David Deutsch's *The Fabric of Reality* (1998) and Brian Greene's *The Fabric of the Cosmos* (2004) are perhaps the most illustrious examples of this tendency. Deutsch's book applies the "fabric" metaphor when aiming to develop an understanding of reality as based on quantum mechanics, considering the subatomic level as the most fundamental. Quantum theory, however, is notoriously difficult to integrate with an Einsteinian physics in a comprehensive view. String theory, which provides the framework of Greene's book, is a proposal to do exactly that: an effort to see together the small scale of particle physics and the large scale of general relativity in a coherent picture. For Greene, it is in the latter context, that of Einsteinian general relativity, that the "fabric" metaphor works best. "Einstein," says Greene (2004: 69), "understood that gravity itself must be nothing but warps and curves in the fabric of spacetime."

Our Element is nevertheless not about the fabric of spacetime, the mysteries of the universe, quantum mechanics, or string theory. Nor do we want to address the question of the "nature" of time by trying to situate approaches to time in physics and the natural sciences, on the one hand, and approaches to time in the human and social sciences, on the other. Although this would be an intellectually exciting and perhaps also necessary endeavor for time studies, our goal in this Element is somewhat more modest. We simply borrow the "fabric" metaphor from theoretical physics in order to make sense of something else. Instead of studying the nature of reality, the building blocks of the universe, and the fabric of spacetime, we aim to explore the fabric of historical time.

To see why it makes sense to approach the theme of historical time with the help of the "fabric" metaphor, the first step would be to get a firm grasp on what historical time is. Most approaches to historical time share a fairly regular assumption, namely that, unlike the time in spacetime – which refers to time as the fourth dimension as combined with the three dimensions of space – historical time is inseparable from human experience. The notion of historical time refers to time not as an abstract and homogeneous entity, but as a dynamic and contextualized constituent of human life, shaped by historical events, social and political structures, and cultural norms.

Reinhart Koselleck (2004: 1–2), the most prominent scholar of the theme in the second half of the twentieth century, explicitly defines historical time as opposed to what he sees as a unitary and measurable natural time. This provides the background of Koselleck's (2004: 2) far larger claim about the intrinsic plurality of historical time(s):

> Even the singularity of a unique historical time supposedly distinct from a measurable natural time can be cast in doubt. Historical time, if the concept has a specific meaning, is bound up with social and political actions, with concretely acting and suffering human beings and their institutions and organizations. All these actions have definite, internalized forms of conduct, each with a peculiar temporal rhythm. One has only to think (keeping to everyday life) of the annual cycle of public holidays and festivals that punctuate social life, or of changes in working hours and their duration that have determined the course of life and continue to do so. What follows will therefore seek to speak, not of one historical time, but rather of many forms of time superimposed one upon the other.

The quoted passage makes clear two things at once. First, it testifies how profoundly the received view of historical time emphasizes its social character; second, it plays out the extent to which change in the sociopolitical domain takes place in diverging paces. The latter aspect is currently a true attention magnet. The intricacies arising out of the recognition of the multiple temporalities and the variety of the intersections of processes that unfold in time with different paces and tempos are among the cornerstones of recent discussions on historical time (for instance, Browne 2014; Jordheim 2014; Esposito 2017; Fryxell 2019; Tamm and Olivier 2019; Landwehr 2020; Edelstein, Geroulanos, and Wheatley 2020a; Bashir 2022; Fareld 2022a). Much of this Element will also be devoted to an examination of such intricacies. What needs to be addressed at this point is, however, not as much the multiplicity of times as the reverse question of why it nevertheless does make sense to talk about historical time, at least historically, as a prominent and once dominant category – without the need of constantly clarifying that what we mean by the singular grammatical form is in fact a plurality of times.

   For underlying the plurality of temporal rhythms and the diverging paces of multiple processes and developments in a variety of human endeavors, there has been a shared conception of history as a developmental process unfolding in time. History as a unitary concept, the idea of a historical process that encompasses all the particular processes and developments, emerged in Western Europe between the mid-eighteenth and the mid-nineteenth centuries. Koselleck has called this period *Sattelzeit* (cf. Décultot and Fulda 2016), meaning practically the formation of the modern world (modernity) through conceptual transformations that shaped the perception of reality. According to Koselleck, the period witnessed the temporalization of a cluster of interrelated concepts. "Revolution," for instance, derived from the circular movement of stars, has achieved a temporal dimension in the *Sattelzeit*. It attained a directionality in time, pointing onward to a desired future (Koselleck 2004: 23).

Most importantly, the desired futures of revolutions and utopias – and, for that matter, any sort of "progress" – have been rendered possible by the simultaneous emergence of the temporalized concept of history as a unitary process unfolding in time. Past and future have emerged as differentiated categories (Schiffman 2011; Hölscher 2016). Or, to use the categories of Koselleck (2004: 255–275), in the *Sattelzeit*, a gap began to form between the "space of experience" (roughly speaking, that which one has experienced in the past) and the "horizon of expectation" (that which one can expect of the future) – and this gap is constantly growing as the "space of experience" and the "horizon of expectation" are moving away from each other at an accelerating pace.

History, the temporalized concept as the Western world came to know it in the past two centuries or so, bridges this gap and smooths the differentiated past and future into a larger trajectory. In bringing new and old together and seeing both as part of the very same process (Arendt 1961), the modern conception of history and its historical time domesticate experienced novelty and expectations of the future (Simon 2019a: 20–27). As soon as the new is seen in familiar lights, as soon as it is conceived of as the next stage in a development of a past potential, radical novelty is tamed. It is one of the great conundrums of historical time that it entails both a rupture in time – as Aleida Assmann (2020) highlights – and the bridging of that rupture through its work of domestication (Simon 2021). Section 1 will explore these perplexities in details. Two more relevant questions need to be asked right after recounting the dominant view on the emergence of historical time: first, *where* is historical time; second, *when* is historical time? Whereas the first question situates historical time on the local-global spectrum, the second addresses both the dating and the historicity of historical time itself. In reality, the two questions often presuppose each other. Studying the historical thought of imperial China (Ng and Wang 2005) or the relation between ancient and modern Western historical thought (Lianeri 2011) implies both questions at once.

That said, for the sake of simplicity, let's begin with addressing the question of where exactly historical time is by having a look at its conceptual environment. In that regard, the links between historical time and the notion of modernity seem evident. As the latter is one of the most frequently deployed and, at the same time, one of the most contested concepts of the human and social sciences, we cannot delve deeply into debates surrounding the notion of modernity. What we would like to point out in this regard is only that due to the intertwinement of modernity and historical time, it is little wonder that critiques of them are also often interlinked. In fact, when addressing the question of historical time, a whole set of interrelated notions is at stake. Consider the following passage from Dipesh Chakrabarty's *Provincializing Europe* (2000: 7):

> Western critiques of historicism that base themselves on some characteriza-
> tion of "late capitalism" overlook the deep ties that bind together historicism
> as a mode of thought and the formation of political modernity in the erstwhile
> European colonies. Historicism enabled European domination of the world in
> the nineteenth century. Crudely, one might say that it was one important form
> that the ideology of progress or "development" took from the nineteenth
> century on. Historicism is what made modernity or capitalism look not
> simply global but rather as something that became global *over time*, by
> originating in one place (Europe) and then spreading outside it. This "first
> in Europe, then elsewhere" structure of global historical time was historicist;
> different non-Western nationalisms would later produce local versions of the
> same narrative, replacing "Europe" by some locally constructed center. It was
> historicism that allowed Marx to say that the "country that is more developed
> industrially only shows, to the less developed, the image of its own future."

Modernity, historicism, progress, development, capitalism, nation and nation-alism, global and globalization – are all heavyweight concepts with complex intersections. Yet all too often they have been seen as adding up to a relatively simple story of "first in Europe, then elsewhere," the one that Chakrabarty highlights as the very structure of "global historical time." Is this the case? Is historical time necessarily Eurocentric? Or is the kind of historical time Chakrabarty refers to only one particular European iteration of historical time, often disguised in the cloak of universalism?

In the third decade of the twenty-first century, it is a commonplace that a uniform conception of historical time, associated with certain experiences in a few Western countries, does not do justice to the variety of experiences of time. While it is evidently true that temporal experiences are many, the question remains whether specifically "historical" conceptions of time are varied too. On the one hand, and on a smaller scale, conceptions of lived time along identity categories in relation to history are increasingly gaining visibility. From feminist multilinear and multidirectional reconceptualizations of historical time (Browne 2014), through nonnormative "trans temporalities" (Devun and Tortorici 2018), to an "oppositional racial chronopolitics" guided by "race as a recognition of the racial structuring of the modern world and the concomitant need for corrective racial justice" (Mills 2020: 312), plenty of efforts set out to problematize the interrelated complex of historical time and Western modernity. On the other hand, and on a larger scale, the booming of localized time conceptions and time experiences poses the question of their relation to the dominant conception of historical time, which they all consider oppressive and from which they attempt to break free. If the problem is the whole historical time/ Western modernity complex, do these efforts then constitute alternative notions of "historical time," or are they better seen as efforts aimed at the recognition of notions of time other than "historical"?

The central normative question of today's debates on historical time is whether we should see only one "historical time" of global aspirations – one that is necessarily of the spatialized developmental structure of "first in Europe, then elsewhere" as Chakrabarty phrased it – or a multiplicity of localized historical times. The politics of both options have potential pitfalls. Whereas opting for the former risks denying a sense of historicity of their own from cultures outside the West, opting for the latter risks considering practically any temporal configuration that relates past, present, and future in one way or another as "historical."

As a case in point, consider the jointly written book of Velcheru Narayana Rao, David Shulman, and Sanjay Subrahmanyam: *Textures of Time: Writing History in South India 1600–1800* (2003). The book's opening sentence immediately sets the stakes by asking: "Did history and historical consciousness exist in South India before the conquest of the region by the British in the closing decades of the eighteenth century?" (Rao, Shulman, and Subrahmanyam 2003: 1). In answering the question affirmatively, the authors of *Textures of Time* intend to challenge what they see as dominant positions in postcolonial studies at the turn of the millennium. This means, on the one hand, the view that associates with history "practically any text that dealt with the past"; on the other, it means views that "history was entirely alien to the authentic Indian conception of things" (Rao, Shulman, and Subrahmanyam 2003: xi). As an advocate of the latter view, the book explicitly mentions Ashis Nandy (1995), who famously argued that there is only one conception of history that has engulfed the globe and sought alternatives to this conception of history by embracing the milliard ways of ahistorical constructions of the past. *Textures of Time* (Rao, Shulman, and Subrahmanyam 2003: 3) counters both views and makes the case for seeing a body of texts "from folk-epic to courtly poetry (*kāvya*) to variously categorised prose narratives" as history. It argues that in South India, prior to the consolidation of colonial rule, "no single genre was allotted to history writing" as was the case in Europe at the time of the professionalization of history as a discipline in the late eighteenth and early nineteenth centuries. According to Rao, Shulman, and Subrahmanyam (2003: 4), history can occur in a variety of genres and in any genres both history and nonhistory can be written, which allows them to see forms of history different from the standards of European professionalized history writing. Eventually, in trying to distance itself from the views of Nandy that there is only one historical time, and thereby from the risk of denying a sense of historicity outside the West, *Textures of Time* opens up to the opposite risk of allowing practically anything to be seen as history.

We do not think that this situation can satisfactorily be resolved. At the same time, it seems to us that both Nandy and the authors of *Textures of Time* base their claims in one or another sense of historicity, which leads us directly to the second aspect we would like to highlight in this introduction, namely that historical time is itself historical. Whatever we think historical time may be is itself subject to change over time. On the one hand, this means that, in a constructivist view, at some points in the past historical time did not exist (as is the assumption of Nandy) and/or was conceived differently (as is the assumption of Rao, Shulman, and Subrahmanyam). In this sense, periodizations and debates on dating phenomena are intrinsic to the history/modernity complex (Davis 2008; Lorenz 2017; Friedman 2019). Little wonder that Koselleck's periodization of the *Sattelzeit*, as well as the dating of practically all individual aspects related to the *Sattelzeit* thesis, has been the subject of intense critical discussions (Jung 2010/11; Landwehr 2012; Décultot and Fulda 2016). On the other hand, the historicity of historical time also entails that it will be differently conceived in the future, and, at some point, it will even cease to exist as a pattern of thought. Hence the fact that we use Koselleck's definition only as an entry point to a larger discussion centered around the claim that the modern configuration of historical time studied by Koselleck has been challenged more recently by other configurations of time. To a large extent, this Element is devoted to the task of fleshing out how, by the turn of the millennium, the once-dominant conception of modern historical time has come to be seen as only one of many coexisting configurations of historical time.

Most importantly, the historicity of historical time is one of the reasons we think that, in 2023, the "fabric" metaphor can shed a new and rather peculiar light on the topic. In that, it even has a great advantage as compared to the other two popular metaphors that occur with equal frequency in thinking about the intersections of time and history: "order" and "regime." Like the "fabric" metaphor, talking about "the order of time" attributes a certain comprehensiveness and coherence to the temporal constitution of reality – be that reality a physical one (Rovelli 2018) or a social one (Pomian 1984). The same applies to the notions of "regimes of historicity" (Hartog 2015) and "time regimes" (Assmann 2020) or "temporal regimes" (Torres 2022), which perhaps are the most historically minded.

The "order" and "regime" metaphors, however, cannot escape the connotation of being enforced. They tend to imply an originary nonorderly state of things on which order is imposed in the constellation of a regime. Perhaps this is why they dominate thinking about time in the social realm while the "fabric" metaphor seems to lack such connotations and seldom makes its way into the same vocabulary. And that is precisely why we co-opt it. By borrowing a metaphor from the sciences, we want to hint at two things at once. First, we intend to align the way we think about historical time with the collapse of the distinction between natural time and historical time upon which Koselleck's investigations have been based. Second, we wish to emphasize the extent to which the recognition of this collapse emerges out of the recent work of the sciences and to situate thereby the scientific "fabric" metaphor with human and social scientific thinking about historical time.

The premise of all this is provided by the notion of the Anthropocene, as it has emerged in Earth System science (ESS) in the past decades, or, more precisely, emerged together with the formation of ESS as a new scientific knowledge formation (Steffen et al. 2020). Since Paul Crutzen used the term at a conference in 2000 to indicate how the Holocene may no longer be the appropriate name for the current geological epoch, the Anthropocene was quickly diffused across disciplines. Behind its more recent multiple appropriations, critiques, and countless conflicting alterations in the human and social sciences (cf., for instance, Haraway 2016; Moore 2016; Davis and Todd 2017; Horn and Bergthaller 2019; Merchant 2020; Thomas 2022), the Anthropocene as an ESS notion intends to capture the systemic collision of the physical/natural and human/social worlds by seeing human activity as one of the subsystems comprising the integrated Earth System (Steffen et al. 2016; Zalasiewicz et al. 2021).

Etymologically, the notion consists of the words "human" (*anthropos*) and "recent" (*-cene*), spotlighting that the stratigraphic findings of late reflect human activity observable in recent sediments.[1] That said, the most attention altogether has likely been paid to the chronostratigraphic aspects of the concept. In a debate across disciplines, the question whether the Anthropocene constitutes an epoch either in Earth history (on the geologic time scale) or in human history (in periodizations of social change) tends to overshadow the far more crucial question of how modern knowledge formations can even comprehend what Chakrabarty (2021: 26) claimed, namely that "anthropogenic explanations of climate change spell the collapse of the humanist distinction between natural history and human history."

---

[1] Human and social scientific criticism nevertheless tends to coin alternative terms on the assumption that *-cene* would mean "age" and the Anthropocene would mean "human age."

True enough, many indigenous ways of living never knew such a distinction. As Cristina Yumie Aoki Inoue (2018: 27) says, for the Yanomami, living in the northern Amazon region, "the forest's biological, cognitive, and physical diversity and the relationships between soil, water, animals, humans, and spirits constitute the very fabric of their lives," in which "there is no dichotomy between nature and society or between land and ways of life." In a similar way, Tamara Bray (2018: 269) argues that pre-Columbian Andean peoples, aboriginal inhabitants of the area of the Central Andes in South America, "were highly cognizant of the fact that persons, places, and things existed within multiple temporal frameworks." Nor was such a dichotomy always present in European thought. Carolyn Merchant's classic *The Death of Nature* (1980) has already shown how the Scientific Revolution slowly displaced an organic view of nature in favor of a mechanistic view in which nature was subjected to human domination. Merchant's own ecosystem thinking, just as well as the more recent ESS view, problematizes and moves toward collapsing the nature/society or nature/culture distinction by focusing on their relation in a systemic frame. So does (without the systemic frame) the anti-anthropocentric imperative of the human and social sciences that has been emerging in a variety of shapes in the past decades across a diverse set of approaches and disciplines, from new materialism (Coole and Frost 2010), through critical posthumanism (Braidotti 2013, 2019), to historical studies (Domanska 2010) and anthropology (Crist and Kopnina 2014).

At the same time, it must also be clear that just because contemporary scientific thinking, human and social scientific imperatives, past thought patterns in Europe and indigenous knowledges can be seen as occupying a vaguely defined platform of decentering the human in one way or another (Tamm and Simon 2020), they do not really talk about the same things. What they all clearly indicate, however, is the necessity to rethink historical time (Tamm and Olivier 2019). They demand that we ask whether it is possible to meaningfully relate the historical time that we tend to associate with human history and the conceptions and scales of time that the modern sciences and various societal knowledge economies used to address in the past centuries.

It is in order to open up to such possibility and to accommodate the scientific impulse and the variety of recent imperatives that decenter the human (without losing sight of the more traditional ways of thinking about time and history in regard to the human world) that our Element will set out to explore the fabric of historical time, including cracks in that fabric and its changes over time. In a four-step argument, it will make comprehensible the momentous leap from modern historical time (that Koselleck investigated) to the ways in which Anthropocene and planetary temporalities recalibrate the fabric. The first step will sketch the basic premises of modern historical time and the exhaustion of these premises in the second half of the past century. The second step will explicate and zoom in on the multiple temporalities and historicities of historical time. The third step will address the consequences of affirming the multiplicity of historical times: if pluritemporality is integral to the fabric of historical time, it follows that the many coexisting temporalities intersect, clash, and conflict in various ways. Finally, the fourth and last step will briefly revisit in light of the preceding discussions the constitution of the fabric of historical time.

1 Modern Historical Time and Its Exhaustion

It is no news that modern historical time (that is, the "global historical time" of Chakrabarty, mentioned in the Introduction), its central features, and its satellite notions have acquired a bad reputation in many scholarly environments. Linearity, developmental processuality, teleology, and the notion of progress have received innumerable criticism in the past more than half century. Being held responsible for promoting the idea of "first in Europe, then elsewhere" and providing thereby the ground for the implementation of violent colonization projects, one might expect that conceptions of modern historical time and practices implying it are by now hard to come by.

Quite the contrary! The open repudiation of modern historical time in intellectual circles has been accompanied by a broad range of practices in society and the scholarly community alike that attest to its continuing appeal. To mention only two, think of, first, the retained omnipresence of progress thinking from economics to party politics. As Tyson Retz (2022) has recently argued, the idea of progress comes in several shapes. The undeniable decline of belief in what Retz (2022:16) calls "absolute progress" – that is, "the idea that progress in separate domains of human endeavor amount to overall human progress," "a totalizing conception of human history" – has been accompanied by the rise of "everybody's progress" (Retz 2022: 37–46) in neoliberal policies pursuing statistical planning and economic growth in the second half of the past century. And such forms of progress thinking reign today, even when they are known to cause disastrous consequences, as shown by Julie Livingston's (2019) analysis of "self-devouring growth" in Botswana, predicated on the implementation of technological solutions that eventually led to reverse effects.

Second, the central tenets of modern historical time reign even in its own criticisms. Decoloniality, both as a theory and as a practice of "decolonization," is modern historical time put to work at its most elemental. It conceives of the present as the outcome of deep historical processes as they unfold out of past patterns of colonial expansion, extraction, conquest, and resistance.

Nothing indicates better the close ties between modern historical time and decolonial thought than the family resemblance of their respective actionable modalities: historicization and decolonization. The same way as practically any present phenomena can be historicized by seeing them within larger patterns of historical processes, practically any present phenomena – from the discipline of sociology (Connell 2018; Meghji 2021) to the Anthropocene (Davis and Todd 2017; Whyte 2017; McEwan 2021) – can be subjected to decolonization and can come thereby to be seen as being molded into their present shapes in the course of specifically colonial historical processes (to which they themselves have contributed).

Does this mean that there is no escape from the hold of modern historical time? Well, no, it does not mean anything like that. It only means that breaking with it may be harder than previously thought. And, perhaps most importantly, it also means that we need a bit more intellectual honesty in openly discussing whether, in spite of all criticism, modern historical time *should* be escaped in the first place. For the emancipatory imperatives of many of today's social move-ments and politically engaged forms of scholarship simply rely on it the very same way decolonial theories and practices do. They cannot but assume that betterment is possible over time in the shape of developmental process and gradual empowerment. This is precisely what nineteenth-century nation build-ers assumed too in the service of constructing national identities (Berger 2022: 34–38). Behind a difference in what counts as a desirable future to build, they share with today's emancipatory imperatives the background assumption of modern historical time.

To hint at the complexities entailed by the survival of modern historical time, in the coming pages of this section, we will discuss its central features. Yet we will do so only in order to foreshadow its relative downfall. For there is a double twist here: it is not only that modern historical time survives despite its many critics, but also that it nevertheless loses its dominance despite its survival. What makes this possible is less the countless intellectual critiques and more the emergence of a variety of practices conceived as having been informed by temporal configurations other than the processual character of modern historical time. These recent challenges and alternative temporal configurations have been theorized in several ways in the past decades, and we will provide a necessarily limited overview of conceptual efforts that range from "presentism" (Hartog 2015) to our own notion of "disconnective futures" (Simon and Tamm 2021). We will do so in order to set the stage for Section 2 by claiming that, together with the survival of modern historical time, they all are part of a larger frame of multiple temporalities and historicities that constitutes the fabric of historical time today.

As a point of departure, we would like to discuss critically, and to modify substantially, what Aleida Assmann (2020: 92–147) considers as the five central presuppositions of the modern time regime: temporal rupture, the fiction of beginning, creative destruction, the invention of the historical, and acceleration. In our discussion, we are going to address a few reigning misconceptions in historical time scholarship, recast Assmann's claims, and condense our own into the following three tenets of modern historical time:

- The dialectic of change and persistence over time, of continuity and discontinuity, of temporal rupture and temporal domestication.
- Future orientation.
- Operationality on all scales.

Before proceeding to the discussion, however, it seems important to point out that Assmann's claims, like those of Koselleck, are confined to Western modernity. What's more, the context of these claims is overwhelmingly Germany oriented. True enough, German territories were the cradle of historicism and the developmental-processual historical time of modernity in the late eighteenth and early nineteenth centuries. Given the close ties between historicism and modernity, Chakrabarty's (2000: 7) claim that "historicism enabled European domination of the world in the nineteenth century" and Nandy's (1995: 46) claim that this "historical consciousness now owns the globe," Assmann's strong focus may even come in handy for our purposes of fleshing out the core features of the kind of modern historical time that has risen to global dominance in the past two centuries or so – often at the expense of other conceptions, as we have suggested.

Let's then begin with a critical reassessment of what Assmann (2020: 93–105) considers the most fundamental: temporal rupture. The differentiation of the temporal registers of past, present, and future enabled the decoupling of what one experienced in the past and what one expected of the future. Plainly put, the future started to appear different from the past. Or, to recall how Koselleck (2004: 255–275) phrased it, the gap between the "space of experience" and the "horizon of expectation" has opened up, perceived novelty has begun to occur, and the future has opened up to change that could even be facilitated. Yet, in pointing at early twentieth-century Western literature and futurist movements to demonstrate how this has been experienced as a break with the past, Assmann pays attention to only one side of a hypothetical coin. In doing so, she associates practically all forms of differentiating between past and future with "rupture." This eventually results in rushed claims such as "the modern time regime does not rely on continuity; it relies on change" (Assmann 2020: 97).

Measured against two centuries of historiographical production, which, according to Eelco Runia (2014: xiii), is "amazingly smart, and brilliantly creative, in chasing monstrous discontinuity away and establishing continuity," Assmann's claim sounds rather odd. For modern history and modern historical time are nothing other than the structuring of time lived as a series of ruptures into a meaningful flow of experience. They are a reconciliation of continuity and change in historical processes on the small scale and in the idea of a unitary historical process on the large scale. As Walderez Ramalho (2020) recently argued, in times of crisis, the experience of time is rather that of disruption and action, complementing the dominance of chronological time. On another level, however, modern historical time is both simultaneously. It is temporal rupture and, at the same time, the "temporal domestication" of that rupture by the integration of experienced and expected novelty into historical processes (Simon 2019a). It is neither discontinuity nor continuity but both, smoothed eventually into a "processual temporality" (Simon 2019b) that integrates change and persistence over time in the idea of a historical process. Hence, our modified first central tenet of modern historical time is *the dialectic of change and persistence over time, of continuity and discontinuity, of temporal rupture and temporal domestication*. It synthesizes the seemingly opposing concepts and experiences of time into a meaningful temporal construct of a process.

The second fundamental tenet of modern historical time that we would like to single out is *future orientation*. François Hartog (2015: xviii) put this both eloquently and bluntly in remarking that "the West has spent the last two hundred years dancing to the tune of the future – and making others do likewise." Or, in the poetic phrasing of Javier Fernández-Sebastian (2016: 125), while discussing the discovery of the future in the Hispanic world, "parallel to the diffusion of the political and historico-political ideologies of the nineteenth century, the future took pride of place on the altar of time as the genuine idol of the moderns." Assmann's second and third points – the fiction of beginning and creative destruction – address this theme from a very specific angle and with different emphases. Assmann (2020: 105–126) highlights, first, the way in which the differentiation between past and future enables new beginnings, and second, how these new beginnings and the pursuit of novelty often entail the destruction of the old. While these most certainly bring to light crucial points, we want to emphasize the larger picture, within which such aspects are indeed characteristic of modern historical time, but they constitute only one form of future orientation, that which implies a radical break with the past in the shape of a "rupture," as discussed earlier.

In reality, however, very few differentiations of past and future entail the radicality of a "rupture," the destruction of the old, and new beginnings.

As Daniel Woolf (2021) has argued, conceptions of change in the modern period vary on a scale. The variety of such conceptions entails conflicting views about the question of how to arrive at the future and what constitutes a desired future in the first place. New beginnings and destructions of the old as implied by the French Revolution or the futurist movement constitute only one form of future orientation in a far larger and more diverse pool. Spreading across the ideological spectrum, the ways to arrive at desired futures in modernity are in fact plenty: progress, revolution, reform, incremental improvement, and gradual stages of development, to name a few. From ideas of radical utopian societies to conservative streams of thought, the pull of the future seems unavoidable to the modern mind. Even postrevolutionary reactionary thought is future oriented, as in the case of currents following the French Revolution. While their desired futures are idealized images of the past, they aim to arrive at that past in the future. Another prominent example is the self-branding of conservatives in the so-called Hungarian Reform Era (1825–48) as *fontolva haladók*, roughly translated in English as "prudent progressives."

Yet the pace of transformation of modern lifeworlds could hardly have been confined. Acceleration accounts for this dynamic, being the last entry on Assmann's list and also a central theme of Koselleck (2004) – one that, as we shall see in Section 2, Hartmut Rosa (2013) has even turned into a theory of modernity. They all see modern historical time as one in which, fueled by the advancements of technology, the gap between past experiences and future expectations is growing at an accelerating pace. This contention compels us to address one of the most frequent topoi and potential misconceptions of historical time scholarship: linearity. In critiques of the history-modernity-globalization complex, the assumed linearity of the modern conception of history and historical time looms large, and linear conceptions of history seem to be what everyone hopes to refute and overcome. However, if acceleration can also be a characteristic of modern historical time, none of these efforts seem necessary or indispensable. For where there is acceleration, there is no linearity anyway, and vice versa. Acceleration is a nonlinear, exponential trajectory, as shown in the "Great Acceleration" graphs (Steffen et al. 2015a), showcasing a simultaneous mid-twentieth-century exponential runaway of both socioeconomic (such as paper production or international tourism) and Earth system trends (such as the atmospheric concentration of methane or ocean acidification).

Pointing at accelerationist conceptions is not to say that modern historical time cannot be seen as linear. It is only to say that it is neither linear nor exponentially accelerating as such. *Some* modern conceptions of historical time may indeed be linear, while, as our example shows, others see accelerating changes informing historical processes.[2] The key component to notice here is that in both linear and accelerating versions, change is conceived of as taking place against the backdrop of a *processual continuity* that underpins change (Simon 2019b).

The processuality of both linear and accelerating conceptions of historical processes provides the basis of the third tenet of modern historical time that we want to underscore: its *operationality on all scales*. The studies of the historical dynamics of Earth, of life on Earth, and of human beings were institutionalized in the nineteenth century as the respective scientific disciplines of geology, biology, and history. They have jointly been part of what one of us has called "the modern project of historicizing nature and the human world alike" (Simon 2020: 15–17). Archaeology has been institutionalized as the study of the human past that predates the focus of disciplinary history on the availability of textual evidence (Frieman 2023). At the same time, geology, biology, and history have been responsible to sketch the historical development of the planet, of life on the planet, and of human societies. Although each of them has relied on their own methods, they all have contributed to the formation of modern historical time. Most evidently, the case is so with the nineteenth-century rise of the evolutionary theory, even if, according to Vassiliki Betty Smocovitis (1992), its adoption turned biology into a unified autonomous discipline only in the twentieth century. Like the modern historical view on the human world elaborated by the emerging discipline of history, the evolutionary view configures the relation between past, present, and future in terms of developmental processes concerning life on Earth.

Although modern historical time has been operational on all scales from Earth history to human history, it has been so only separately. As Staffan Bergwik and Anders Ekström (2022: 1) have recently remarked, "not only human societies but also landscapes, species, and the layers of the earth were increasingly temporalized in the nineteenth century, but within different fields and practices, creating multiple timescales and divisions between the rhythms and paces of nature and culture." These disciplines have become institutionalized on the premise of a distribution of work, each focusing on its own scale. Against this backdrop, the question of scale gains a new importance in today's Anthropocene discussions (Thomas 2014; Veland and Lynch 2016; Oppermann 2018; Dürbeck and Hüpkes 2022). However, if the necessity to situate the deep time of geology and the Earth System within the temporalities of the human world seems troubled, it is not because some of these times are not "historical,"

---

[2] An exponential view of change increasingly takes root in technological and entrepreneurial discussions (Kurzweil 2004; Azhar 2021). We will return to this briefly in Section 2.

but rather because of the assumed separation of the scales in which historical time has been presumed to operate in modernity. As the later sections will delve into these difficulties more profoundly, for the moment let us focus on the complexities related to human historical time.

On the human scale, the developmental processuality and the future-oriented character of modern historical time highlight social and ethico-political dimensions. Let us recall an earlier remark by Hartog (2015: xviii) that "the West has spent the last two hundred years dancing to the tune of the future – and making others do likewise," especially its latter part. The first aspect to note in this respect is what Koselleck (2004: 246) describes as the "contemporaneity of the non-contemporaneous, initially a result of overseas expansion," which "became a basic framework for the progressive construction of world history." In a different shape, we have already met this in Chakrabarty's characterization of "global historical time" as "first in Europe." Elaborating on the point, however, Chakrabarty (2000: 8) famously described the modern temporal constellation nurtured by historicism as one that "consigned Indians, Africans, and other 'rude' nations to an imaginary waiting room of history."

Next, the global reach and expansion of modern historical time entailed a variety of "temporal comparisons" (Steinmetz, Simon, and Postoutenko 2021), which, in the colonial context from Latin America to India (Grosfoguel 2000; Banerjee 2006; Dube and Banerjee-Dube 2006), typically boiled down to notions of backwardness and underdevelopment as relative to those who lead in a worldview based on conceiving of the world in terms of developmental processes. Modernization efforts and policies to "catch up" with historical development have, however, also underpinned more recent events. From the modernization challenges in East Central Europe after the fall of communist regimes – modernization challenges that, as László Laki (2021: 272) argues in the case of Hungary, incited social dynamics throughout the twentieth century that could not adequately be captured by invoking the ready-made analytical categories of Western scholarship – to the extremities of an intensely paced "compressed modernity" (Kyung-Sup 2022) of post–Second World War South Korea, modern historical time has been mobilized in various ways.

Finally, as probably the most prominently spotlighted ethico-political dimension of modern historical time, twenty-first-century scholarship on colonialism brings to light the excess of violence as an integral feature of colonialization and colonial rule. With the attention to violence, the question of complicity comes to the fore too. Cheryl B. Welch (2003), for instance, addresses the individual level by putting to scrutiny Tocqueville's rhetorical strategies to evade and tone down such complicity. Priya Satia (2020) raises the stakes by arguing that the function of conscience management to justify the colonial violence of the British empire was, to a large extent, fulfilled by a historical imagination engaged in discussions of noble ends of progress.

Needless to say, these three fundamental tenets do not exhaust the complex arrangements of modern historical time. The ones that we highlighted – the dialectic processuality of change and continuity, future orientation, and operationality of all scales – are the ones at the center of the arguments of more recent theories that argue that modern historical time has already lost its dominance and is being challenged by alternative temporal configurations.

While modern historical time continues to inform a variety of societal practices and discourses – from economic growth imperatives to decolonial thought – its hold on a broader range, let alone the entirety of such societal practices and discourses, is increasingly loosening. Again, what we mean is less the fact that it has been hard for the past few decades to come by explicit endorsements of linearity, teleology, progress, and so forth in scholarly discussions: by now, being critical of such notions is an intellectual commonplace across the Westernized human and social sciences. More compelling in regard to a recognition of tears in the fabric of modern historical time is the perception of a growing number of new temporal configurations in contemporary societies. At the same time, more comprehensive cultural analyses argue that the contemporary world has been leaving behind the modern temporal constellation by shifting to a novel one.

To start with these comprehensive cultural analyses, perhaps the most prominent is Hartog's (2015) argument about a shift in "regimes of historicity" (we will return to this concept in Section 2). According to Hartog, the future-oriented modern regime of historicity is phasing out and a new presentist one – with its sole viewpoint in the present – has been coming to prominence since around the end of the Cold War. A similar diagnosis was first proposed by Helga Nowotny (1988) when she argued that the temporal category of the future is being abolished and replaced by that of the "extended present" (see also Nowotny 1994: 8, 51). In addressing the "broad present" as a new chronotope, Hans Ulrich Gumbrecht (2014) also talks about something very similar to what Hartog (2015: 201) describes as the present being "extended both into the future and into the past." Finally, entering a discussion with Hartog's and Gumbrecht's analyses, Aleida Assmann (2020) takes issue with their pessimistic outlook. Assmann considers the recent attention to the present survival of past injustices and the collapse of strict temporal barriers between past, present, and future as a welcome fixing of modernity rather than the supersession of the modern time regime.

Regardless of their differing positions, however, all these cultural analyses reflect on the same contemporary phenomena, and all are necessarily confined by the fact that their reflections arise out of their experiential horizon of their own Western cultural (and national) environments. It nevertheless remains true that the new societal practices they single out rewire present relations to the past and the future, within and outside the scope of these theories. On the one hand, the rise of memory studies, heritage discourses, and reparations politics, as well as the prominence of questions revolving around transitional justice, historical injustice, and the manifold legacies of colonial wrong-doings, rewire relations to the past. On the other, new and potentially runaway technoscientific and anthropocenic prospects, discourses and practices – ranging from transhuman aspirations aimed at breaking out of the biological confines of being human to anthropogenic Earth System transformations and a human-induced mass extinction of species – entail relations to the future that cannot be adequately conceived of within the frame of modern historical time and cannot be fully captured by analyses of presentism either. Let us take a closer look at both.

An emerging new temporality of the changing relations to the past breaks down the temporal barriers between past and present (Bevernage and Lorenz 2013). In the past decades, several conceptual innovations attempted to capture a past-present relation that calls into question the temporal distance between time registers that characterizes modern historical time. The notion of "presence" and the broader discourse on the presence of the past (Gumbrecht 2004; Bevernage 2008; Lorenz 2010; Ghosh and Kleinberg 2013; Runia 2014: 49–83) have likely gathered the most attention in historical theory (we will return to this notion in Section 2). But does the growing attention paid to presence of the past entail a countermovement of diminishing attention paid to the future? In a volume exploring reparations of historical injustices, John Torpey (2003: 1) claims that "so pervasive is this phenomenon that 'coming to terms with the past' in contemporary politics has extensively supplanted the elaboration of visions of the future." In a recent book fully embracing modern historical time, Olúfẹ́mi Táíwò (2022) makes the case for what he calls a constructive view of reparations associated with a future-oriented outlook aimed at a just distribution of historically accumulated advantages. The implied transitions from the distributive injustice of the present (accumulated from the past through conventional historical processes) to distributive justice are relatively modest, and the book's vision of the future is less a positively stated utopia and more a negatively defined freedom from past injustices.

Again, when it comes to the question of the future, does this mean that the only choice left is between a pessimism about the possibility of positively stated futures on the one hand and a return to modern historical time and its processual future orientation on the other? Not really. At least it doesn't mean anything like that when we look outside the explicitly political domain and look beyond everyday politics, where a structural transformation of conceiving the future is taking place, dominantly in technoscientific and anthropocenic practices. The novelty of the most extreme future imaginaries of what we call "disconnective futures" (Simon and Tamm 2021: 7–8) is the temporal disconnection they posit between past and future.

Before dismissing the importance of these imaginaries as mere speculation, let's not forget that modern historical time has been premised on imaginaries of future sociopolitical conditions. For the structure of modern historical time and for the modern historical sensibility, it never mattered that sociopolitical development had never actually reached the stage of classless societies for instance. What mattered was the conceivability of such prospects and the plausibility assumed by their advocates. Accordingly what we want to point out is not that anticipated anthropocenic and technoscientific futures will actually take place. Our point is that the conceivability and assumed plausibility of structurally new kinds of futures emerge in today's technoscientific prospects, and that they are informed by new kinds of historical times.

However, the interrelation of the temporal constellations of a large set of societal practices can be extremely complex. How do any of the technoscientific temporalities relate to a temporal anxiety of what Anne Fuchs (2019) calls "precarious times" or to the growing concerns in academia for the recognition of indigenous temporalities (Reid, Sieber, and Blackned 2020)? To foreshadow our answer, which we will explicate in detail in Section 2, we would like to invoke Stefan Tanaka's (2019) call for a "history without chronology." As a counterintuitive phrase, it immediately grabs attention. Yet, in equating chronology with linear time and claiming that it forecloses the many temporalities otherwise given at any time and place, Tanaka's analysis eventually turns out less radical than it seems. It even remains indebted to a processual view of modern historical time. On the other hand, we think that its argument for a more liberating view that should enable us to see a multiplicity of historical processes unfolding at different paces resonates closely with the growing pluralist sentiment in time studies. Most importantly, it also implies an answer to the question of what to make out of the oftentimes conflicting interpretations we have just touched on.

It seems to us that much of the aforementioned views do not negate one another but form a complex web of interrelations within a frame of multiple temporalities. Although seeing them together may indeed entail contradictions, conflicts, and aporias, these are, we believe, intrinsic features of the pluritemporality of historical times. Section 2 will delve into the intricacies of the multiplicity of times, mostly in regard to its more recent constellations.

2 A New Multiplicity of Historical Times

We all live and have always lived in different times. "The baseline for human existence on Earth is that we are out of sync with each other, as well as with our surroundings, simply because we live in a condition of multiple, heterogeneous, and diverging times," as Helge Jordheim (2022a: 47) has recently put it. The idea of a homogenous and universal time is a modern myth (Hamann 2016), or, more exactly, as we will see, a felicitous act of temporal synchronization. But we have to bear in mind that this myth or act of synchronization has never been exclusive. Ever since the emergence of modern historical time, there has been a strong alternative tradition of thinking in terms of the coexistence of multiple historical times. This tradition goes back to the early days of modernity, to Johann Gottfried Herder, Friedrich Schleiermacher, Karl Marx, Wilhelm Dilthey, and others.

As a most illustrative and still topical early example, think of how Koselleck (2004: 2, 237) made widely known the emphatic words that Herder aimed at Kant in his *Metacritique of the Critique of Pure Reason* (1799):

> In reality, every mutable thing has its own inherent measure of time; this would persist even if no other were there; never do two things in the world have the same measure of time. My pulse, my step, or the flight of my thoughts is not a temporal measure for others; the flow of a river, the growth of a tree cannot be the measure time for all rivers, trees, and plants. Lifetimes of elephants and of the most ephemeral are very different from each other, and how different are not the temporal measures on all planets? In other words, there are (one can say it earnestly and courageously) in the universe at any one time innumerable different times. (Herder 1998: 360, quoted by Jordheim 2022c: 409).

Theoretical thinking of time in plural has been particularly prolific within the Marxist philosophical tradition (Tomba 2013). Harry Harootunian (2015: 23) even argues that Karl Marx was "the first to see and record the experience of the past as constantly intruding in the lived present, thus persuading him of the necessity of negotiating the multiple temporalities of non-contemporaneity individuals must always confront in their daily lives." Marx used the model of plural temporality to explain the different developments of European nations. He was particularly interested in the non-contemporaneity of German philosophy with respect to German society and its contemporaneity with the historical developments of France and England (Morfino 2018: 146).

At the same time, it must also be clear that more recent views would not condone the politics of time in Marx. As Nandy (1995: 46) remarks, "everyone knows" that "Marx thought of Asiatic and African societies to be ahistorical.

Few know that he considered Latin Europe, and under its influence the whole of South America, to be ahistorical too." In a sardonic sentence, Nandy (1995: 46) concludes that "after banishing so many races and cultures from the realm of history, the great revolutionary was left with only a few who lived in history – Germany, where he was born, Britain, where he spent much of his later life, and the Low Countries through which, one presumes, he travelled from Germany to England."

For the modern Western mind, however, ahistoricality was not the endgame. It expected the whole globe to enter a historical condition through the onward march of a world-historical process (Guha 2002). This compels us directly to address right at the outset the question of a specifically historical time as a unitary developmental process unfolding over time with a potentially global scope. For it is one thing to critique the assumed unitary character of historical time in European traditions, and another thing to address how even such critical traditions may remain inattentive to integral dimensions of the workings of historical time in regards to its spatial aspects. Modern historical time, the whole package, the spatiotemporal construct with a global scope, divided the world between those who lead development and those who lag behind.

Western history, modernity, and coloniality as its "darker side" (Mignolo 2011) were hanging together in producing not only coexisting multiple temporalities but also practices and discourses of "catching up" across the globe, from Latin America to Eastern Europe. The tradition of thinking time in plural in Europe that we delve into in a bit more detail – flourishing especially in German-speaking intellectual environments – must be seen not only in regard to what it actively advocated but also in regard to that which, recent human and social scientific scholarship knows better in hindsight, it was either unable to conceive or it actively overlooked at best and oppressed at worst.

Among these is the very tradition of thinking time in plural outside the West. Islamic time, for instance, as most brilliantly explored lately in the ground-breaking digital endeavor of Shahzad Bashir, *A New Vision for Islamic Pasts and Futures* (2022), belongs to that tradition. Alongside the possibility of conventional chapter-by-chapter reading, the web interface of the book enables readers to access sections of the books through a visual table of contents that consists of a map of the sections arranged as a web, which, upon hovering over any section, highlights the other sections (across different chapters) with which the selected section is linked.

This format already exemplifies the book's approach to the relation between Islam and temporality. For instance, in what would constitute the first section of the second chapter, Bashir (2022) zooms in on the religious complex in Kudus, Indonesia. Whereas the conventional approach of modern historical time would

integrate it into a timeline and see it as "derivative, a latter-day Javanese Jerusalem exhibiting Muslims' investment in the holiness of a city in the Middle East," Bashir suggests to begin "Islamic history in Java and then catapult away to other places, times, and themes that have their own multi-layered stories." To do so, Bashir (2022) needs to replace the idea of history as "a homogenized, uninterruptible vector" and the view of a "single arrow of time" with "multiple, heterogenous temporalities whose inner logics are not universals driven by anonymous causality." In light of the argument that Islam was "timelined" in the nineteenth century – embedded in a Western historical time and its standardized chronology of progression (which does not mean denying that such temporal progression was one of the multiple temporalities available across Islamic genres) – Bashir presents Islamic history as web of intersecting multiple lines without "predetermined directionality."

Back in Western Europe, however, the multiplicity of historical times has meant something other than a web, being more closely related to the view of history that – to use Bashir's expression – "timelined" other temporal experiences. In the early 1930s, Marxist philosopher Ernst Bloch compellingly conceptualized the coexistence of multiple times as the "non-contemporaneity of the contemporaneous" (*Ungleichzeitigkeit des Gleichzeitigen*). A critique of uniform time can be found in all of his philosophical production, from *The Spirit of Utopia* (1918) to *Experimentum mundi* (1975), but it is in *Heritage of Our Times* (1935) that this topic moves into the foreground (Morfino and Thomas 2018: 10). "Not all people exist in the same Now," writes Bloch;

> They do so only externally, through the fact that they can be seen today. But they are thereby not yet living at the same time with the others. Instead they carry earlier elements with them; this interferes. Depending on where someone stands physically, and above all in terms of class, he has his times. Older times than the modern ones continue to have an effect in older strata. (Bloch 1985: 104, translated by Schwartz 2001: 58)

Bloch's theory of non-contemporaneous times emerged out of the contemporary German discussions in the history of art, and more specifically, from the work of Wilhelm Pinder. "There is no simple 'present,'" observed Pinder eight years before *Heritage of Our Times* appeared, "because every historical 'moment' is experienced by people with their *own* different senses of historical duration; each moment means something different for everyone – *even a different time*" (Pinder 1926: 15, translated by Schwartz 2001: 62). Bloch adapted the concept of *Ungleichzeitigkeit des Gleichzeitigen* from Pinder in order to explain German history in the aftermath of the First World War, and in particular the formation of Nazism. For Bloch, the multiplicity of times was an ontological statement.

He held that instead of a single time, we should talk about a temporal "multi-versum" (Bloch 1985: 104; see Bodei 1979), while emphasizing at the same time that there is also a multiplicity of ways of imagining time.

Within the Marxist tradition, the theory of multiple temporalities was further elaborated by Louis Althusser in the early 1960s, particularly in his *Reading Capital*, written with some of his students. Althusser's aim was to develop an alternative to the "ideological conception of historical time" (Althusser and Balibar 1970: 96). With this in mind, he proposed a model of relationality and dislocation (*décalage*) that constitutively prevents the identity of the present with itself, revealing its presumed unity to be a real plurality (Thomas 2017: 282). According to Althusser, "the structure of historical existence is such that all the elements of the whole co-exist in one and the same time, one and the same present" (Althusser and Balibar 1970: 94). Each of these historical occurrences is "punctuated with peculiar rhythms," but it is not sufficient to think they coexist only in their differ-ences: "we must also think these differences in rhythm and punctuation in their foundation, in the type of articulation, displacement and torsion which harmonises these different times with one another" (Althusser and Balibar 1970: 100). Arguing against the existence of a singular notion of historical time, for Althusser, historical time needs to be thought of as an articulation of plural temporalities without common measure (cf. Osborne 1995: 23–29; Bevernage 2016: 14–16).

It is against the background of this rich philosophical legacy that we should read Koselleck's influential theory of historical times, which brought the ques-tion of pluritemporality into the limelight of contemporary historical theory. True enough, Koselleck doesn't refer to this earlier philosophical tradition; rather he invokes French historian Fernand Braudel as a pioneer in conceptual-izing historical inquiry as multitemporal (Koselleck 2000: 12–14). As is well known, in the 1950s, Braudel criticized the standard uses of temporality in history and argued for a tripartite model of historical time that foregrounds the *longue durée* (in relation to the conjunctural time of social structures and the short term of political events) as the methodological ground for a unified historical social science. "Whether it is a question of the past or the present," Braudel (1958: 727) claims, "an awareness of the plurality of social time is indispensable for a common methodology shared by the human sciences." Braudel constructs his model of multiple historical times in terms of three temporalities. First, the *longue durée*, the longest conceivable historical temporality; second, cyclical time or the conjuncture, a structural time of intermediate duration; and third, the event or the (very) short term (cf. Harris 2004; Sawyer 2015).

But we should notice an important difference between Braudel and Koselleck. While Braudel's temporalities were arranged according to scale, from the slow-moving geological and geographical structures down to the singular event, Koselleck conceives of historical time in terms of overlapping layers of temporal patterns. His approach opens the possibility of nonsynchronous synchronicities, different historical times coexisting in the same present, rather than a pyramidal hierarchy of levels. "To Koselleck the key word is not multiplicity or plurality," as Helge Jordheim (2014: 504) succinctly explains, "but *Ungleichzeitigkeit*, nonsynchronicity." It is also worth mentioning, as Juhan Hellerma (2020) has recently pointed out, that Koselleck engaged with the idea of multiple temporalities not only on a theoretical level but also as a practicing historian. His *Habilitationschrift* in 1967 was explicitly informed by the insight on the plurality of overlapping time layers, as we can read from the book's introduction: "[T]he account corresponds to the different levels upon which historical movement unfolded. From a theoretical perspective, it deals with different layers of historical time" (Koselleck 1967: 14, quoted by Hellerma 2020: 194).

By now, especially in the past decade, it has become the majority view in historical theory and in theoretically inspired historical scholarship that history writing reveals a coexistence of multiple times. Jordheim has been one of the most vocal proponents of this approach. Based on a close reading of Koselleck's work, Jordheim (2014: 500) points out that "globalization has brought with it more complex and heterogeneous temporal relations, in which the global time of commerce, technology, and media comes into conflict with the different rhythms in the variety of cultures and communities." On the other hand, the "deep times" of climate change and of the Anthropocene challenge the limited temporal horizons of social relations and political decisions and force us to redefine our relations with the past and future.

In the wake of Bloch and Koselleck, and in agreement with Jordheim, we argue in this Element that multiple temporalities are integral to historical time. At the same time, it seems to us that the multiple temporalities framework sees only one part of a far larger fabric, to recall the metaphor we introduced earlier. Hence our main contention is that *the fabric of historical time consists of complex interactions not only of multiple temporalities but also of multiple historicities*. Accordingly, we base the work of this section on a conceptual distinction we make between *temporalities* and *historicities*. While discussions of historical time tend either to conflate the notions of "temporality" and "historicity" and use them interchangeably or to leave undertheorized their respective conceptual shapes and relations to each other, we think that such a distinction is crucial to gain an understanding of the fabric of historical time as a multiplicity of temporalities *and* historicities.

By temporalities we have in mind various *modes of being in time*, the rhythms of existence that are immanent to the very processes of material being itself in all its manifestations. This comes close to the line of thinking of Russell West-Pavlov in his book *Temporalities*, in which he proposes that "time is nothing but the vibrant, pulsing dynamic of life itself: a time immanent to the constantly changing being of things. This time-in-things, however, is not merely that of humans, but of all life, whether animate or inanimate, organic or inorganic" (West-Pavlov 2013: 48). By historicities we understand various *modes of change over time*, or, more precisely, the ways individuals and groups conceive the transitions across time, their ongoing social production of accounts of meaningfully relating pasts, presents, and futures (Hirsch and Stewart 2005: 261, see also Bantigny 2013: 15–16; Hartog 2015: 16; Baschet 2022: 186). Although temporality and historicity remain overlapping notions to a large extent, the distinction is crucial in acknowledging that – due to the temporal transition characterizing conceptions of historicity – all historicities imply temporalities, but not all temporalities imply historicities.

Based on this conceptual distinction, the remaining pages of this section will be divided into two main parts: one will explore main contemporary forms of temporalities, from sociopolitical to more-than-human temporalities, while the other will discuss the variety of contemporary historicities or some new ways of articulating pasts, presents, and futures. To prepare the ground for these discussions, however, the more immediate task consists of mapping the current conceptual toolbox designed to make sense of multiple timescales.

Figures of Historical Time

Thinking historical time in plural is a genuine conceptual challenge. When we give up the idea of a single uniform historical time, we are confronted with major conundrums, starting with the need to pluralize all forms of our temporal vocabulary. Chris Lorenz (2021) has lately made this point very clear: "In a pluriform temporal universe *no one* – including historical theorists – is allowed to claim anything by just referring to '*the*' past, '*the*' present and '*the*' future, because '*the*' past, present and future *only exist in the plural*." It is therefore not surprising, as Victoria Fareld (2022b: 27) recently acknowledged, that "a lot of intellectual effort today is thus invested in reinventing and enriching the temporal terminology, in order to provide historians with a more useful conceptual toolbox." We will try to cover in the coming pages this complex ground in three steps. First, we shall discuss various conceptual renderings of *configurations of time* – that is, terminological efforts to capture the coexistence of different historical times. Second, we will focus on *spatial figures of time*, on attempts to make sense of pluritemporality with the help of spatial metaphors. And third, we will explore the *spectral figures of time*, some more psychologically oriented conceptual endeavors to come to terms with the non-contemporaneity of the contemporaneous.

Probably the most successful term for the configuration of historical time in recent years has been *regime*. In the field of historical time studies, the term was introduced by François Hartog (2015) in his book *Regimes of Historicity*. Using this analytical tool, Hartog sought to capture temporal configurations in which one of the three registers of past, present, and future dominates the other two. In Hartog's approach, the term "regime" encompasses three different layers of meaning: the dietary regime, the political regime, and the regime of the winds. "What these relatively disparate domains have in common is the idea of degrees, of more or less, of mixtures and composites, and an always provisional or unstable equilibrium," he contends (2015: xv). Although Hartog has always insisted on the heuristic function of the "regime of historicity," by pairing it with the hypothesis that the current regime of historicity is that of "presentism" in which the present dominates the other two temporal registers, the concept has acquired, especially in subsequent elaborations, an ontological quality with regard to the human historical condition (Lorenz 2019; Mudrovcic 2021).

Even in its heuristic use, the concept of the regime of historicity presupposes a certain unity of articulations of time within the limits of a regime. This aspect of the regime as a unifying frame has attracted criticism from various angles. For instance, Peter Burke, in his study of early modern temporalities, has proposed to redefine regimes of historicity as internally diversified realms in which distinct temporalities encounter one another. "The theory of regimes needs to find a place for both continuities between regimes and for variation within them," Burke argues (2011: 54). In a similar way, Jérôme Baschet (2018, 2022) has suggested that any discussion of a regime of historicity can only refer to a leading tendency, which may not be exclusive: "In some societies, one regime of historicity may be largely dominant or even almost exclusive, whereas in other contexts there may be a more marked competition between distinct regimes of historicity, and sometimes a lesser cohesion of them, or even a proliferation of multiple relations to historical time" (2022: 185). Finally, from a sociological perspective, Felipe Torres has recently argued in analogous terms that the diversity of temporal structures, not only in their historical succession but also horizontally in their simultaneous coexistence, is the main missing aspect in Hartog's notion of regimes of historicity. "The definition of *regime* has the potential for considering more than one pattern of regularity," Torres (2022: 22) writes:

> In this sense, it is possible to think simultaneously of various regimes interacting with each other, as well as the struggles in-between and inside of them. By doing this, we can identify patterns of acceleration coexisting with "slow food" movements; a measurable-standardised global time in parallel with sacred, mystic and non-rational temporal ideas; futurist perspectives with presentist or romantic paths; urban vs rural paces; as well as differentiations by gender, age or even employment.

Therefore, the question is whether it is possible to empirically substantiate the argument that certain temporal articulations – regimes of historicity or temporality – dominated certain periods, or would it be more adequate to consider that for most periods in history, several temporal regimes coexisted side by side? The latter approach is taken, for instance, by Achim Landwehr (2020: 43), who argues that societies do not live in the "cocoon of a monolithic time regime," but cultivate numerous time forms that coexist in a "world of pluritemporality" (*Welt der Vielzeitigkeit*). According to Landwehr (2016: 288), past and future are not separate ontological domains, but coexist as projections of the present: "For pasts were not and futures will not be as we describe them, but all these times exist, and they do so, actually, simultaneously." To analyze the flow of relations between times that are absent and those that are present, Landwehr (2016: 149–165; 2018: 239–265) introduces the concept of *chronoference*. In his definition, chronoference signifies the "ability of collectives to refer to absent times and to produce a culturally specific web of timings" (Landwehr 2018: 266). The intersection of multiple time relations in the present forms a complex "time-scape" (*Zeitschaft*) as Landwehr (2016: 281–316) calls it. "There is no escaping this complexity," Landwehr (2020: 24) argues, "because even if we should wish it, the times will not do us the favor of lining up neatly and tidily." Chronoferences can take a wide variety of forms, transgressing by far the boundaries of historical research. "Every planning for the coming day, every life insurance policy, every look at the photos from the past vacation, every look at the weather forecast and every story that begins with the words 'Do you still remember . . . ' evokes such a chronoference" (Landwehr 2020: 247).

In the wake of Landwehr, but with a different emphasis, Dan Edelstein, Stefanos Geroulanos, and Natasha Wheatley have recently proposed yet another new figure of time to understand pluritemporal relations, that of *chronocenosis*. Taking its inspiration from the ecological term of "biocenosis," which refers to various forms of cooperation, adaptation, and conflict within and between the populations of a particular biosphere, chronocenosis is "a way of theorizing not simply the multiplicity but also the conflict of temporal regimes operating in any given moment" (Edelstein, Geroulanos, and Wheatley 2021b: 4). Chronocenosis creates the possibility of introducing the perspective of power in temporal relations and provides, according to its authors, "a sense that multiple temporal regimes are not merely concurrent but at once competitive, conflictual, cooperative, unstable, and sometimes even anarchic" (Edelstein, Geroulanos, and Wheatley 2021b: 27). This is indeed an important addition to the previous conceptual discussions, and we will return to the conflictual character of time relations in Section 3.

Anticipating the call of Edelstein, Geroulanos, and Wheatley, Jordheim (2014: 510) has proposed that "in our discussion of multiple temporalities we should not content ourselves with describing pluralities or multitudes but move on to discover the contrasts, oppositions, conflicts, and struggles involved in structuring, regulating, and synchronizing time." In his view, the foremost power of time lies in the ability to adapt and adjust different times, or, to put it briefly, to synchronize them. An order of *synchronization* is, according to Jordheim, a shared temporal framework with which people align and adapt their own individual times.

Synchronization is a social and performative phenomenon requiring a great deal of "work of synchronization," or, by reference to Niklas Luhmann, an "act of synchronization" (Jordheim and Ytreberg 2021: 404). Jordheim and Einar Wigen (2018) have recently proposed that *crisis* has become in the Western world the main conceptual tool for carrying out such "work." In their view, the emergence of the crisis is linked to the emergence of presentism; the crisis is not pointing to the future, but to the present as a site for great transformations. "To replace a multitude of crisis concepts, from different parts of human and natural life, with one concept, one collective singular *crisis*," Jordheim and Wigen (2018: 435) contend, "means adjusting and aligning a whole range of temporal experiences and structures, such as crisis as periodic iteration, crisis as permanent condition, and crisis as the end of the world as we know it." This comes close to the idea of *chronic crisis* Anne Fuchs (2022) recently suggested. In her approach, the contemporary notion of "crisis" no longer designates the experience of a decisive tipping point after a climactic buildup, but rather an enduring state of extremity requiring uninterrupted resilience.

All that said, at the most fundamental, we argue that the very creation of a modern homogenous and uniform concept of historical time amounts to a felicitous act of synchronization. In this sense, the entire modern Western notion of historical time as a developmental process unfolding across the globe, and thus the modern Western idea of history as such, can be seen as a result of synchronization. On the one hand, as several generations of criticism hold, centuries of colonialism have imposed Western conceptions of time and space over the world – including the synchronized time of the Western idea of history (Conrad 2018). On the other, however, as Boaventura de Sousa Santos (2009: 104) points out, "some versions of the achievements of the West managed to impose themselves internally, at the same time that they imposed themselves on the rest of the world." This means the modern idea of history as a unitary process unfolding over time is a synchronized temporal construct imposed on a multiplicity of time within and outside the West.

Sverker Sörlin (2022) has recently proposed that we have witnessed three main waves of temporal synchronization in the modern era. The first was the introduction of progressive historical time around the turn of the eighteenth century. The second focused on standardizing practices and infrastructures for universalizing time in the second half of the nineteenth century, and the third refers to the integration of different temporalities across the entire disciplinary spectrum into an emerging geo-anthropological or Anthropocenic temporality (see also Sörlin and Isberg 2021). Jordheim and Ytreberg (2021), concurring with this last point, have proposed that the concept of the Anthropocene has been in the present century the main conceptual tool for the synchronization of different timescales.

Another main avenue for rethinking historical times in plural has been the use of *spatial figures of time*. In the introduction to his essay collection *Zeitschichten*, Koselleck asserts that every attempt to theorize time depends on the use of spatial metaphors. We can think about time only in terms of space, as "the metaphorical power of all images of time emerges initially from spatial notions" (Koselleck 2000: 9). Koselleck's own preference, as we noted, was to talk about the "layers" or "sediments of time" (*Zeitschichten*). With this conceptual metaphor he aimed to grasp historical time as multiple and layered in a stratigraphic manner; history unfolds as an interaction between time layers pressed together but occurring at different speeds, rhythms, and duration:

> "Layers of time," just like their geological prototype, refer to several temporal levels (*Zeitebenen*) of differing duration and varied origin that are nonetheless simultaneously present and effective. Even the contemporaneity of the non-contemporaneous (*die Gleichzeitigkeit des Ungleichzeitigen*), one of the most revealing historical phenomena, can be brought under a common denominator by "layers of time." (Koselleck 2000: 9)

Koselleck's aim was, therefore, to circumvent the linear–cyclical dichotomy characteristic of historicist thinking, claiming that "historical times consist of multiple layers that refer to each other in a reciprocal way, though without being wholly dependent upon each other" (Koselleck 2018: 4; see also Jordheim 2014; Hellerma 2020).[3] In a recent critical reading of Koselleck's stratigraphic model of multiple times, Chris Lorenz (2022: 214) has observed, however, that this model does not really explain how to identify and account for layers of historical time and therefore "will remain at best a seductive metaphor in history."

Cultural semiotician Juri Lotman provides a much less-known example of spatial thinking of multiple times. In the late 1980s, Lotman elaborated his inventive semiotic theory of history, based on the idea of historical unpredictability and heterotemporality (Tamm 2019, 2022b). "Real historical processes are multi-layered and poly-functional, and, as a result, can be described in different ways from different points of view," wrote Lotman (2019: 98) in 1992. For him, "history is not a unilineal process but a multi-factored stream" (Lotman 2019: 184) made up of temporal layers that develop at different speeds. In the same way, Lotman conceptualized culture as a complex whole "created from elements which develop at different rates, so that any one of its synchronic sections reveals the simultaneous presence of these different stages." Rapid changes in some layers of culture may be combined with gradual development in others. "This, however, does not preclude the interdependence of these layers" (Lotman 2009: 13).

More recently, a new attempt has been made to think across human and natural temporalities in terms of *timescales*. In the eponymous collective volume, editors Bethany Wiggin, Carolyn Fornoff, and Patricia Eunji Kim explain that the timescale concept registers their desire "to foreground the deep time (liveliness, experience, agency) of nonhuman processes":

> Timescales reject man as the measure of all things ... Timescales understand temporality as a simultaneously material and discursive premise with its own weight or mass, modeled in ways that disclose certain kinds of information while diminishing other perspectives ... timescales foreground a mode of critical attunement to ecological change that encompasses expansive categories like landscapes, species, class, and race, interrogating their interconnectedness and how they take shape at different rates. (Wiggin, Fornoff, and Kim 2020: xiii–xiv)

Over the recent couple of decades, a more allegorical and psychological way of addressing the multiple temporalities has led through the *spectral figures of time*

---

[3] Harry Harootunian (2015: 21) remarked that Koselleck's "layers of time" resemble the "stadia-lized" pasts (*jūsōsei*) of the Japanese philosopher Watsuji Tetsurō (1889–1960): stratigraphic layers imposed on each other represent in his approach a vertically organized inventory of past epochal traces. Watsuji, who studied briefly with Martin Heidegger, inverted Heidegger's emphasis on Being's authentic historicality (time) by proposing the importance of environment – climate and place (space) – as a determining mediation in shaping human and specifically Japanese life.

like "afterlife," "hauntology," and "presence," which represent the third cluster of figures of time we would like to indicate. Jan Assmann (1997: 9) has neatly captured the idea: "The past is not simply 'received' by the present. The present is 'haunted' by the past." This way of thinking seems to stem also from Marxist tradition. Already in *The German Ideology* (1846), Marx and Engels proposed the concept of a past constantly seen as mingling with the present, "depositing in every present its residual traces that embodied untimely temporalities announcing their unevenness and difference" (Harootunian 2015: 17). Marx formulated this idea most memorably a few years later in *The Eighteenth Brumaire of Louis Bonaparte* (1852):

> The tradition of all the dead generations weighs like a nightmare on the brain of the living. And just when they seem engaged in revolutionizing themselves and things, in creating something that has never yet existed, precisely in such periods of revolutionary crisis they anxiously conjure up the spirits of the past to their service and borrow from them names, battle cries and costumes in order to present the new scene in world history in this time-honoured disguise and borrowed language. (Marx 1972: 10)

One important conceptual figure of time in this context is the German term *Nachleben*, made popular by Aby Warburg in the early twentieth century. This concept, which is rather difficult to translate into English, should be understood as a continued life, the past that becomes actual in the present, or the past that haunts the present. Therefore, instead of the traditional "afterlife," a more appropriate translation might be "survival" or even "revival" (Tamm 2015). The term *Nachleben* was not coined by Warburg himself; it can be encountered on several occasions in the works of German scholars during the second half of the nineteenth century, but thanks to Warburg it has become one of the key concepts in contemporary humanities. As Georges Didi-Huberman (2002: 55) brilliantly demonstrated, *Nachleben* is a term that enables Warburg to show the complexity of historical time, to set out how "the past is woven of many pasts." According to Warburg, we are living within a symbolic *Nachleben* of the past, within this multilayered and haunting dynamic of presence and absence, which continually influences our historical imagination and understanding. The Warburgian idea of *Nachleben* is also the point of departure for Dan Karlholm's (2018) recent proposal to rethink historical time in art history. Turning a key causal factor of conventional history – influence – around, he proposes to think along the lines of *outfluence*. "This way to historicize a work of art," Karlholm (2018: 17) writes, "would entail focusing not on what it once was and how come, but on what it has *become*."

Another spectral figure of time – "hauntology" (*hantologie*) – originates from Jacques Derrida's book *Specters of Marx* (1993). Composed of two words – haunt and ontology – the concept of hauntology refers to a study of the role of ghosts or specters in the shaping of history – "the persistence of a present past or the return of the dead" (Derrida 2006: 101). In Derrida's view, inspired by Marx, the present is never synchronous to itself; it is always haunted by the ghosts of the previous periods. He calls into question the traditional articulation of historical time and proposes to open the "spectral spaces" otherwise closed in linear temporality. Berber Bevernage, one of the first to use a Derridean spectral conception of time in historical theory, explains well its importance for rethinking historical time: "The specter, therefore, is not just a piece of the 'traumatic' past popping up into the present; rather, its logic questions the whole traditional relationship between past, present, and future" (Bevernage 2008: 163; see also Bevernage 2011: 19).

Ethan Kleinberg argues in the same vein that the concept of hauntology opens a possibility for historians to investigate the presence of the past without having to recur to a metaphysical conception of historical reality. In his book *Haunting History*, Kleinberg (2017: 132) combines Derridean hauntology with the notion of the non-contemporaneity of the contemporaneous, contending that this approach accommodates "an understanding of the past as something that is, as present *and* absent at the same time, as something *and* nothing entangled in a seemingly impossible way, where the iterative position of the historian is woven into the past and the present such that it also presses on the future." In brief, hauntology becomes a theory of multiple times that all converge on the present. Or, in an even more unconventional manner, hauntology could become a form of historiography, through experimenting with conflating times and bringing ghostly presences to the process of writing, as in the experiments of Margrit Pernau (2019; 2021: 12–18).

The final conceptual figure we have selected from the same semantic family for our necessarily incomplete survey is *presence* (cf. Bos 2021). The strongest advocate of this concept in history and philosophy of history discussions, Eelco Runia, argues that in order to reestablish contact with the reality of history, "we should forget about the things that came to pass and had better focus on the living on of the past in the here and now" (2014: 147). Runia uses the concept of *presence* to refer to the subconscious persistence of an unacknowledged past: "In presence, the past is present in the here and now in much the same way as in transference the past of a psychoanalytic patient is present in the psychoanalytic situation" (2014: 100). For Kleinberg (2013: 1), another advocate of the "presence" approach, this concept helps to understand "the ways that the past is literally with us in the present in significant and material ways"; it marks "a return to a relationship with the past predicated on our unmediated access to actual things that we can feel and touch and that bring us into contact with the past."

Similarly, for Frank Ankersmit (2006: 335), presence refers "to this stubborn persistence of the past in which it remains a presence in the present."

All in all, in our overview, we have focused on the largest-scale figures of time that comprise the analytical toolbox of studies of historical time. Time figures are, however, everywhere, and the study of such figures as they occur in societal practices and discourses is a flourishing stream of (historical) time studies. Modernity produced a great panoply of new figures of time, most of them in service of the homogenous and irreversible notion of time. Lucian Hölscher (2020) recently collected and analyzed some of the most influential modern *Zeitfiguren*. These include *Zeitgeist*, "epoch," "progress," "development," "historical break," and so forth (Hölscher 2020: 211–287). Moira Pérez (2022: 36) calls these and related notions of Western modernity "temporal figurations," defined as the "concrete, varying ways in which time is organized through representations (historiographical or other)." Highlighting their politics, Pérez (2022: 41) contends that "hegemonic figurations effectively assign politically marginalized subjects and collectives to a deferred temporality, therefore displacing them from the present in which their political identity (that is, their identity as political agents) and perhaps their survival are at stake." The figures of time in scholarly work enable, at best, the study of such figurations of time, and we hope that our short overview of the figures of multiple temporalities demonstrated that the conceptual ground is well prepared to rethink (historical) time in plural.

Multiple Temporalities

Needless to say, it would be impossible to cover all variations and transformations of temporal modalities in today's world. What we can reasonably attempt is to illustrate our central argument of the *radical polytemporality* (Helgesson 2014) of our current historical condition by discussing briefly three key arenas: sociopolitical, material, and more-than-human temporalities.

Sociopolitical temporalities. The idea of multiple temporalities is deeply rooted in the sociopolitical realm. Already in 1937, Pitirim Sorokin and Robert Merton published an essay that argued that social time is heteronomous in nature, it does not flow evenly, and it is not freely divisible (Sorokin and Merton 1937: 621–623). Another key contribution to the theory of multiple social times was made by Georges Gurvitch in his book *La multiplicité des temps sociaux* (1958), translated into English as *The Spectrum of Social Time* (1964). Gurvitch's approach, inspired by Maurice Halbwachs's (1950) idea of "multiple collective memories," is grounded in the statement that social life in its various forms flows in different and diverging times, which often compete with each other. "Each social framework," Gurvitch (1964: 151) contends, "produces its own times and often its own scale of times." On the basis of criteria such as duration, method of pulsation, and rhythmicity of movement, he distinguishes eight main types of social time by which the diverse displays of time can be expressed in a sociohistorical manner, from the "enduring time" of slow duration to the "explosive time" of creation (1964: 31–33).

Instead of a typological approach to multiple social times, which reduces the inherent heterochrony to some all-encompassing master tropes, it is our intention to discuss in the following pages some diverging aspects of contemporary sociopolitical temporalities. We propose not to conceive of social time as a universal frame that embraces all phenomena alike; instead, we want to explore the entanglement of multiple times that do not form a homogeneous whole. In this, we will focus on three temporal diagnoses or constellations that have gained some currency in today's research literature: *acceleration*, *presentism*, and the *presence of the past*.

For many scholars, speed and acceleration have come to characterize contemporary sociopolitical temporalities. Concepts such as "timeless time" (Castells 1996), "chronoscopic time" (Virilio 1986), "network time" (Hassan 2009), "pointillist time" (Maffesoli 2003), or "instantaneous time" (Urry 2000) have been proposed to capture the accelerating character of digital and network societies (Wajcman 2015: 14). True enough, the argument that time moves faster than ever before is rather old (cf. Dodd and Wajcman 2017; Bouton 2022). In the early twentieth century, for instance, Georg Simmel (2002) argued that the speed of the modern metropolis, alongside the acceleration of exchange relationships made possible by the circulation of money, was giving rise to a new social temporality. For Koselleck (2004: 40–42, 241–246; 2018: 79–99), acceleration refers to developments distinctive of modernity, constantly shortening the time span within which new experiences can be expected relative to past experiences. More recently, Hartmut Rosa has developed his own influential theory of social acceleration, identifying three sources of the contemporary transformation of social tempo: technological acceleration, the acceleration of social change, and the acceleration of the pace of life. Rosa (2013: 63–73) explains acceleration as quantitative growth or increase in quantity per unit of time. In the case of the pace of life, for instance, this amounts to an increase in the number of episodes of experience or action per unit of time (be it a day, a month, a year, or a lifetime). Complementing the idea that acceleration is reflected in the substantive temporalities of human existence, we find it important to emphasize the great variety in rhythms of acceleration, from social changes to computerized high-frequency trading. The rapid development of digital technology is making increasingly possible new and multiple temporalities, often in conflict with each other (Wajcman 2015).

One of the early theorists of speed, Paul Virilio (2010: 71), has suggested that the main outcome of the social acceleration is that "past, present, and future contract in the omnipresent instant." He called this new temporal situation "instantaneism" (Virilio 2012: 22). With an emphasis other than speed, probably the more successful term for capturing this new mode of being in time has been "presentism," proposed by his compatriot François Hartog.[4] As discussed earlier, presentism refers, according to Hartog, to the contemporary Western experience of time that emphasizes the primacy of the present: "Since it has neither a past nor a future, this present daily fabricates the past and future it requires, while privileging the immediate" (Hartog 2015: 113). The hypothesis of presentism has attracted quite a lot of scholarly notice over recent years, of which we would like to highlight the constructive criticism offered by Jérôme Baschet (2018). Whereas Hartog and others after him defined presentism through a focus on the present and the disappearance of the future, Baschet claims that in the case of presentism, it is more accurate to speak about the birth of new future modalities rather than the vanishing of the future. He emphasizes also that presentism is not the only existing regime of temporality in today's world: "the presentist regime is not imposed unilaterally or homogeneously. It does not reign with the same rigor nor exactly in the same forms depending on whether one considers the large metropolises of the globalized world or the rural areas, the North or the South" (Baschet 2018: 111).

One particularly interesting constellation of sociopolitical temporalities in relation to historical time is the *presence of the past*, as played out especially in the judicial realm. What makes it interesting is that jurisdictional temporality frequently assumes a reversible character, meaning that the criminal would remain forever contemporary with his crimes (Hartog 2015: 201). The main turning point in this legal domain was the European Advisory Commission's decision in 1945 to lift statutory time limitations on the prosecution of crimes against humanity. This inapplicability of time limits was confirmed by the Statute of the International Criminal Court in 1998 (De Baets 2011). Victoria Fareld (2018: 55–56) argues compellingly that this principle of legal impre-scriptibility – the principle that crimes have to be investigated, prosecuted, and punished regardless of the passage of time – has introduced a new notion of time not only within the field of the law but also within the field of history. "It is an act which turns the past into something upon which one can act

---

[4] Ludivine Bantigny (2013: 23) has pointed out that, in 1996, French philosopher Jean Chesneaux had already proposed the concept of *présentéisme*, evoking the withdrawal to the present and "the alienation of the sense of duration."

morally and legally, by letting it coincide with the present in an extended contemporaneity." In discussing Vladimir Jankélévitch's critique of the statute of limitations and the question of whether the expiration of crimes over time could be allowed even in the case of the Nazi regime, Fareld (2018: 61) aligns the time of the victim, a "time that does not pass," with the time of the imprescriptible. In the latter time, continues Fareld, "the chronological temporal scheme that situates the crime as something belonging to the past is simply ruled out"; "the past is reclaimed as an ethical space where past, present and future coincide" (2018: 61).

The conceptual outlook of imprescriptibility, we believe, resembles the temporal constellation also underlying wider debates on reparations (Henry 2003; Táíwò 2022), reconciliation (Barkan 2009), truth and historical expert commissions (Pettai 2018), and transitional justice (Bevernage 2011). Chris Lorenz (2017: 116) observes astutely that these "all revolve around a growing conviction that the once commonsensical idea of a past automatically distancing itself from the present is fundamentally problematical." In this regard, Jankélévitch's thinking has left another conceptual mark on recent studies of historical time, with slightly different emphasis. In contrasting the "time of jurisdiction" and the "the time of history" and criticizing the assumed conflict between the two in terms the reversibility and irreversibility of time, Berber Bevernage (2011: 4–6) sought balance by reviving Jankélévitch's notion of the *irrevocable* to conceptualize a past being stuck in the present.

Material temporalities. Alfredo González-Ruibal (2016) has noticed incisively that the reversible time of jurisdiction has many similarities with the time of archaeology. In the same way as international law claims that crimes against humanity are not subject to any statute of limitations, archaeology denies the past its radical absence and distance by reminding us that it is still present through its vestiges. "In this sense," González-Ruibal (2016: 20) contends, "both archaeology and jurisdiction work in a regime of spectrality, that is, one in which the haunting presence of the past disturbs the present."

One has to admit that the voice of archaeologists has rarely been heard in the discussions of historical time. However, material temporalities, increasingly attracting the attention of archaeologists, constitute the royal road to better understand the complex fabric of historical time. Laurent Olivier (2004: 205) wrote emphatically almost twenty years ago that "from the archaeological point of view, the physical environment of the present is essentially made up of the things of the past, of a more or less recent past, whereas creations of the present moment (of 2004, of this very day) occupy only a tiny place in this physical present which is in fact imbued with the past." And he concludes: "The present has always been multi-temporal and above all has never been young, never totally of the present" (see also Olivier 2013: 169). Christopher Witmore (2006: 279) drew a very similar conclusion two years later: "Archaeological time is the entanglement, the intermingling, the chiasm of pasts and presents."

González-Ruibal (2006) offers a good empirical example of such an approach in his study of a Gumuz village in Ethiopia, where a vast array of artefacts from different parts of the world and different historical moments still coexist, in use, in everyday life: adzes, plastic beads, a digging stick, firearms made in the former Soviet Union and Italy, and many other items. In a more recent study of grave goods in later prehistoric Britain, Anwen Cooper and her colleagues (2022) have explored the multi-temporal rhythms of Neolithic burials in chambered tombs, where rites of rearrangement with both bones and objects extended the temporalities of people and objects. In the same vein, Olivier (1999) has questioned the illusion of synchronicity embodied in the Early Iron Age "princely" burials such as the Hochdorf chieftain's grave in Germany. In his reading, the grave goods from such burials embodied multiple temporalities: power was based on relations that were extensive in space by amalgamating materials of different origins, but also extended in time. Likewise, a recent collective study into the pre-Columbian Andean archaeology concluded that "[t]he physical persistence of the past in the present and the efficacy of buildings and accumulated artifacts to direct future action reveal that 'archaeological time' is dynamic and 'pluritemporal,' one of diverse retentions, protentions, and discontinuities" (Swenson and Roddick 2018: 5).

Next to archaeology, material temporalities also play out frequently in artworks. "No device more effectively generates the effect of a doubling or bending of time than the work of art, a strange kind of event whose relation to time is plural," Alexander Nagel and Christopher Wood claim in their innovative study *Anachronic Renaissance* (2010: 9). Taking up Warburg's idea of a discontinuous, folded historical time, the authors propose to draw from the artworks themselves what they call "a lost chronotopology of art making" (2010: 34). Nagel and Wood demonstrate to what extent each artefact gestures to many different kinds of time and how the complex and layered temporalities of images offer a counterpoint to traditional linear chronologies (for a critical discussion, see Rampley 2022). In recent years, the concept of *pictorial temporality* has gained some currency in scholarly discussions, based on the argument that pictures are entangled with temporality on multiple levels – including in terms of their time of production, materiality, depicted motifs, or perception and reception (Grave 2019; Hochkirchen 2021).

Reflecting on the nature of material temporalities, Ömür Harmanşah (2020: 46) has observed how "deep time" often leaks into the present: "Archaeological time allows us to think about an alternative, nonlinear temporality in which such a leakage becomes possible, through material remains and palimpsests in landscapes. One could call this 'percolating time,' that is, deep time leaking into the present through ongoing material entanglements and spatial proximities." According to Harmanşah (2020: 49), this "percolating time" deconstructs modernism's linear temporality and "replaces it with an understanding that suggests time is a product of relationships, ongoing material entanglements, and spatial proximities." In that regard, material temporalities intersect with a variety of the sociopolitical temporalities of the human world, many of which also defy the modernist-historicist processuality into which conceptions of historical time have often been enforced in the past two centuries or so. Most importantly, however, material temporalities also point beyond the human endeavor. On the one hand, the human world can easily be decentered on cosmic timescales; on the other, decentered human timescales and more-than-human timescales collide precisely in regard to the material temporalities that bind them together.

More-than-human temporalities. The idea of percolating material time, first proposed by Michel Serres (Serres and Latour 1995: 60), points to a new mode of temporality we find particularly important in today's world and would like to dwell on at the end of this overview, namely more-than-human temporalities. The main challenge of theorizing time today is to think of human times together with the times of nature, to open up social and historical time to include other "lifetimes," as Jordheim (2022b: 187) calls these in the wake of Herder:

> The concept of "lifetimes" bridges the nature-culture distinction and replaces the dichotomy of natural time, on the one hand, and social and historical time, on the other, by a continuity of scales. Life – both human and non-human – unfolds at various time scales, from seconds to millions of years, which converge in events and their aftermaths.

The need to go beyond traditional human timescales in the study of historical time is directly related to the emergence and recognition of the Anthropocene predicament (Thomas 2022). The more acute awareness of the role of humans in the Earth System and of geological and climatic processes has given way to a new sense of temporality, allowing us to think of time with an increasingly widening sense of depth into the past and into the future. Calls to reckon with Anthropocene time are plenty. Sverker Sörlin and Erik Isberg (2021: 717) have recently noted that the Anthropocene concept entails "new geo-anthropological temporalities for the human-earth relationship." Almost a decade earlier, Libby Robin (2013: 329) forcefully stated that "the developing idea of the Anthropocene ... demands both geological and historical time-scales, and writes planetary and human histories together." Eduardo Mendieta (2020: 130) concurs: "We should, then, think of the Anthropocene as a temporal revolution, a crisis of human temporalities."

One of the features of this temporal revolution is that it activates and entangles new timescales, often on different orders of magnitude compared to the ones that have been current in political and social realms. However, as Chakrabarty (2021: 156) notices:

> [I]n most [human and social scientific] discussions of the Anthropocene, questions of geological time fall out of view and the time of human world history comes to predominate. This one-sided conversion of earth-historical time into the time of world history extracts an intellectual price, for if we do not take into account earth history processes that out-scale our very human sense of time, we do not quite see the depth of the predicament that confronts humans today.

This separation of the geological and historical timescales is not as old as it is often assumed. According to Fabian Locher and Jean-Baptiste Fressoz (2012), it came into effect only around the end of the nineteenth century. Prior to that, the scales of cosmological, geological, and human time have been seen as homogeneous and entangled. What has changed, however, is the calculation of the age of the Earth, which has passed progressively from 75,000 years according to Buffon's pioneering work of 1778, *Epochs of Nature*, to 4.55 billion years, as established by means of radiometric dating in 1955 by Clair Cameron Patterson (Bouton 2018: 38). The Anthropocene predicament and anthropogenic climate change has marked the reconnection of geological and human scales of time and the waning of the modern distinction between the temporalities of human and natural history. In the introduction to the recent collective volume *Times of History, Times of Nature*, editors Staffan Bergwik and Anders Ekström (2022: 2) argue compellingly that "with growing insights into how human societies act as a major force in geological and atmospheric processes, the idea of human agency as external to floods and rising temperatures is no longer obvious. Neither can nature be conceived of as the slow and repetitive background to historical events."

In the wake of recent scholarly literature on the Anthropocene, we can differentiate between two kinds of more-than-human temporalities, *climate change temporalities* and *anthropocenic temporalities* (Kverndokk, Bjærke, and Eriksen 2021; Ekström and Bergwik 2022). Julia Nordblad (2021: 330) observes that "the Anthropocene and climate change imply two different temporal frameworks, both shaping the way anthropogenic environmental degradation is thought of and debated politically." In her judgment, the concept of anthropocenic temporalities does not support the critical thinking about how the current environmental crisis can be addressed and for forging political action, while the notion of climate change offers a more useful framework for thinking and ultimately acting politically. A more feasible view, however, would contend that anthropocenic temporalities – linked with the larger-scale transformations of the condition of the Earth System that are not subject to our direct experience, rather than with the more tangible effects of climate change – are far from apolitical; they are simply political in ways other than those we are accustomed to, and the challenge today lies with the demand to develop new forms of planetary-scale politics (cf. the diverse efforts ranging from Kashwan 2020 through Iheka 2021 to Chakrabarty 2021). What this means is that these two temporalities have very different scopes. Climate change represents just one facet of the Anthropocene predicament. Or, in other terms, the Anthropocene as an Earth System science concept refers to the entirety of our planet's interacting physical, chemical, biological, and human processes, whereas climate is just one element of this system (Thomas 2019).

The concept of deep time, proposed by John McPhee (1981) and popularized by Stephen Jay Gould (1987), was forged to highlight the disproportion between the geological and human scales of time. However, in our Anthropocene predicament, it is increasingly important to make sense of human life in close relation to deep-time movements, to look at ourselves "in the mirror of deep time" (Grinspoon 2016: x). Richard Irvine (2020: 2) has reminded us to what extent "the material conditions of human existence can be understood only as the product of processes occurring over deep time" and how isolating life from the geological flows "is to distort our understanding of society and of humanity." In resonance with our argument in this Element, Irvine (2020: 18) claims that the key question of today's scholarship is "what is the relationship between human temporalities and the temporalities of the more-than-human world within which humans live?" The conceptual and empirical mapping of these complex relationships is the most challenging endeavor in (historical) time studies.

However, we want to underline that these relations are not defined by deep-time movements alone, but rather by the entanglement of different durations and chronologies. As happily explained by Emily O'Gorman and Andrea Gaynor (2020: 717), "'more-than-human' is not a synonym for 'nature' or 'nonhuman' but, rather, a term that highlights the primacy of relations over entities (including the 'human')." In brief, more-than-human temporalities require a pluralistic and relational understanding of time that is open to its multiple rhythms, events, and trajectories over different scales, from the smallest to the biggest.

Multiple Historicities

Let us begin by recalling the distinction we made earlier between the more general concept of *temporality*, referring to the various modes of *being* in time, and the more specific term of *historicity*, covering the different modes of *change* over time. To enable us to map new modes of change over time, we have recently conceptualized the multiplicity of transitional relations between apprehended pasts and anticipated futures occurring in societal practices and discourses as "historical futures" (Simon and Tamm 2021). Teaming up with the journal *History and Theory*, we have initiated a large project dedicated to surveying such transitional relations in practices and discourses ranging from transhumanist imaginaries (Taillandier 2021) through extinction scenarios (Jørgensen 2022) to the "potential history" of Amerindian indigenous knowledges read together with developments in artificial intelligence (AI) research (Bonaldo and Pereira 2023). Many of these new modalities of "historical futures" differ from the conventional "historical" transitions from pasts to futures, which have typically been configured along developmental processes in the past two centuries. Yet this does not mean that older kinds of transitions have faded out. We rather think that our current historical condition is defined by the simultaneity of such transitions and thus the simultaneity of multiple historicities. That said, to emphasize novelty, in our brief and incomplete survey, we will focus on what we think are newer kinds of historicities and the concepts through which these can be captured.

A central tenet of modern historical time has been, as we have seen, that even though past experiences and expectations of the future parted ways already in modern historical time, they nevertheless remained connected through the assumption of a processual historicity. Today's new ecological and technological prospects, we argue, break with this processuality by disconnecting anticipated futures from apprehended pasts. They conceive of change as "unprecedented change" (Simon 2019a) – that is, a transformation informed by an "evental temporality," in which a game-changer "epochal event" is expected to open up a whole new reality (Simon 2019b; 2020). As an illustrative example of such disconnection, one can think of transhumanist aspirations aimed at escaping the confines of the biological limitations of being human by technological engineering (More and Vita-More 2013). Whereas the paradigmatic project of modern historical time has been the perfectibility of humans over time, the transhumanist endgame concerns bringing about a condition that is not simply a better human condition, but one that is better-than-human (Simon 2019c; Tamm 2022a).

Even though the self-branding of transhumanism tends to emphasize an evolutionary understanding of the historical process, the very aim of transitioning into other-than-human futures points beyond the continuity of self-identity required by evolutionary modes of historical thinking. Curiously enough, the self-branding of human and social scientific theories of the posthuman (MacCormack 2012; Braidotti 2013; Ferrando 2019) testifies to a similarly confusing situation, although in the opposite direction. In associating posthumanism with a critique of humanism and the aim of overcoming anthropocentrism by developing a worldview that sees the human in a web of planetary life, critical posthumanism is typically presented as "radical" transgression. Its posthuman, however, is not a literally posthuman subject but a new human subjectivity, and, as a kind of historicity, it is based on familiar emancipatory conceptions. It appears then, that humanities-oriented and technoscientific discourses and practices of the posthuman represent "two cultures of the posthuman future" (Simon 2019d) precisely because they represent two distinct historicities: one branded as "radical" but in fact theorizing a familiar historical transition to a new human worldview, and one branded as familiar "evolutionary" transition but in fact envisioning a radical breakaway from the human condition.

All that said, it is also clear that there is a massive asymmetry and disparity between these prospects and the perception of the actual taking place of "technofutures." According to Sun-ha Hong (2022), the contemporary status and ubiquity of predictive technologies as prominent forms of contemporary historicity is maintained by ritualized demonstrations of capacities rather than by the actual success of technological predictions and the actual coming about of prophesied outcomes. In a similar vein, Mateus Pereira and Valdei Araujo (2020) argue that a new shape of historical time that manifests in smaller-scale technological practices is what they call "updatism." On the semantic level, they note the emergence of "update" as way of structuring time experiences, filling the void left by the shrinking appeal of "progress." As Pereira and Araujo see updatism as a present-oriented form of historical time, the question of the relation between the temporalities of imaginaries of the future and smaller-scale technological practices remains open. It may very well be that prospects of "unprecedented change" and "presentism" are heavily interlinked and the latter emerges as a response to the former (cf. Hellerma 2021).

We claim that one of the distinctive traits of the Anthropocene predicament and increased technological powers is the plurality of possible transitions from pasts to futures, often radically different from one another. Although modern forms of transition, such as development, progress, emancipation, and revolution, have not disappeared completely and still inform our anticipatory practices, new forms of transition and new concepts to capture these transitions – *transitional concepts*, as we call them (Simon and Tamm 2021: 15–17) – have emerged alongside these more familiar ones, producing new kinds of historicities.

One such new transitional concept was recently proposed by Jérôme Baschet (2021, 2022), namely the notion of "switchovers" (*basculements* in French). He forged this concept to overcome the historicist idea of a single, inevitable trajectory and to emphasize the systemic instability of today's world. Switchovers are "essentially unforeseeable," "broad and massive," and "uncertain in their activation" (Baschet 2022: 195). Baschet explains that a great variety of transitions can be included within this concept: "the abrupt appearance of unprecedented and unexpected situations, threshold effects that involve violent accelerations, sudden turnovers, largescale movements comparable to tectonic shifts, and so on" (Baschet 2022: 195). As examples, one can think about the COVID-19 pandemic or the yellow vests protests in France. The concept of switchovers is characterized by a dual logic: "the rupture brought by the switchover proper and the preceding accumulation that makes it possible" (Baschet 2022: 195). This accumulation should not be understood as continuous. The existing elements are subjected to a reconfiguration that gives them a totally new meaning. "Switchovers," Baschet concludes, "may help us to visualize a nonlinear history that, while discontinuous and attentive to the possibilities, nevertheless honors the imperatives of a reformulated processual approach" (Baschet 2022: 195).

Whereas the notion of "switchover" remains committed to the idea that historical change must be processual at its most fundamental level, the notion of an epochal event (Simon 2020) emphasizes that the most momentous transformations, as they are being conceived in ecological and technoscientific practices and discourses, introduce "temporal incommensurability" between pre-eventual and post-eventual conditions. The reality before the event and the reality after the event have no common measure in terms of having no central subject that could provide a connection between the two times and thus enable the telling of a processual history. The lack of a subject that remains self-identical before and after an epochal event is most apparent in the aforementioned transhumanist scenarios. No processual history can bind together the history of humanity and the history of beings better-than-human and other-than-human: the history of the former is not the prehistory of the latter (Simon 2019c).

The notions of "switchover" and "epochal event" have originally been conceived as working in different registers. Whereas the former is derived from the Zapatista experience and its main operational space in the sociopolitical temporalities, the latter is aimed at making sense of more-than-human temporalities, both discussed earlier. Their locus of conception, however, does not determine their potential use. As any other notion, they are being transferred from context to context, especially as just as many aspects bound them together as those that differentiate them. At their most fundamental, both represent conceptual efforts to come to terms with the emergence of new historicities, and, as such, they highlight different elements of the same complex.

Depending on whether one highlights processual or disconnective aspects, some of the transitions of the Earth System from its past to its future states may, as projected by ESS, qualify as switchovers as well as epochal events, especially those tied with the transgression of climate "tipping points" and "planetary boundaries," upon which complex systems are expected to transition to altered states in a radical manner (cf. Lenton et al. 2008, 2019; Rockström et al. 2009; Steffen et al. 2015b). In a similar way, many transhumanist visions of the future contain an irreversible turning point – called an "intelligence explosion" (coined in 1965 by I. J. Good) or "technological singularity" (popularized in 1993 by Vernor Vinge) – the result of the exponential process of technological progress. This turning point is the anticipated moment when the exponential curve of technological evolution reaches the point where unprecedented and unpredictable changes take place in the blink of an eye. Ray Kurzweil, one of the main promoters of the singularity theory, defines this moment in the following terms: "It's a future period during which the pace of technological change will be so rapid, its impact so deep, that human life will be irreversibly transformed" (2005: 9). All these prospects – from transgressing the planetary boundaries to reaching the technological singularity – are vested with a transformative potential that is far larger than what is commonly associated with modern historical time.

In coming to terms with the Anthropocene, Dipesh Chakrabarty (2021: 23) was one of the very first to draw attention to the new "sense of the present that disconnects the future from the past by putting such a future beyond the grasp of historical sensibility." He noted pointedly that this new situation challenges the modern sense of historicity and the epistemological foundations of historical research: "The discipline of history exists on the assumption that our past, present, and future are connected by a certain continuity of human experience." Eventually, Chakrabarty (2021: 68) has come to the conclusion that "planetary or Anthropocenic regime of historicity" is the adequate term for a new historical sensibility. The notion that Hartog used to capture the possible constellations of temporal registers (constellations in which the past, the present, or the future dominates the other two), Chakrabarty has now employed with reference to the collision of histories of various timescales (human histories of the globe, of biological life, and of the planet).

Chakrabarty is seconded by Hartog in his recent book *Chronos* (Hartog 2022: 233) where he also argues for the emergence of an "anthropocenic regime of historicity," a new way to overcome the various temporal gaps in our life: the gap between the time of the Anthropocene and the times of the world, the gap between digital presentism and the other temporalities of the world, and the gap between digital presentism and the temporalities of the Anthropocene. "It is no longer, as it was in the good old days, a matter of simply articulating past, present, and future," Hartog (2022: 233) contends, "but of taking into account pasts, presents, and futures, whose impacts may differ, diverge, even contradict each other, but which nonetheless form a nexus or a web of temporalities in which, to one or another degree, we act and are acted upon."

Both Chakrabarty and Hartog refer to a new planetary awareness of humanity, considering it a major turning point in human history. In the view of Christophe Bonneuil, however, the idea of planetarity dates back at least to the early nineteenth century. Bonneuil (2020: 73) finds that "the question of whether a new regime of historicity would have emerged at the time of the Anthropocene appears indecisive, even ill-posed if we examine it in its complexity." Instead, he calls for a *longue durée* historical study of planetary thinking, or more precisely of "planetary regimes" – that is, "the historically situated ways in which human societies, thinking about their future, connected the human agency with the agency of other than humans, up to the temporal and spatial scales of the planet" (Bonneuil 2020: 73). On the one hand, this may provide the idea of planetarity with a longer history. Yet, on the other hand, it must be equally clear that such domestication of novelty appeals to the conventional procedures of modern historical time (Simon 2021), seeking to demystify radical novelty by smoothing it into processual histories. The earlier findings of "planetarity" might not have much to do with how, in the view of Chakrabarty (2021:68), "Earth System scientists as historians" are "writing within an emergent regime of historicity."

In striking a balanced note, we would argue that even though linking the planetary or the Anthropocene with a regime of historicity is plausible to a large extent, this does not necessarily mean that the planetary or the Anthropocene could alone constitute such new regime. These are rather the central conceptual tenets of multiple historicities through which we apprehend the world and ourselves historically in times of major ecological and technological transformations. What we need is less to insist on figuring what the single defining feature of a regime may be and more to work toward recognizing the multiple historicities without overwriting them with the processuality of modern historical time and the inherited codes of professionalized historiography (Simon 2021).

Such a recognition would be the precondition of taking the next step and venture into exploring the tremendous complexities in which temporalities and historicities interact. To indicate these complexities, Section 3 will take a closer look at one such interaction: the conflicts of temporalities and historicities.

3 Conflicts in the Fabric of Historical Time

Inasmuch as the fabric of historical time consists of multiple temporalities and historicities, it harbors a relational complexity. Developing an understanding of such complexities should be, ideally, the goal once multiplicity is recognized. However, compared to the frequency of pronouncements of multiplicity and the work devoted to identifying and fleshing out particular temporalities, the attention devoted to the more intricate question of how temporalities intersect and interact remains relatively scarce.

Recent efforts that nevertheless aim to grapple with such relational complexities revolve around two central themes that we have already touched on in Section 2. The first is the synchronization of times and its conceptual counterpart, desynchronization (Jordheim 2014, 2022a); the second is the conflicts of temporalities (Edelstein, Geroulanos, and Wheatley 2020a; Fareld 2019, 2022b). In this final section, we want to bring these two threads of scholarship on historical time into a meaningful exchange by pointing out that time conflicts arise out of the synchronization and desynchronization of temporalities. To put it in a more thesis-like form: our claim in this section is that *conflicts are intrinsic to the fabric of historical time, and such temporal conflicts are derivative of ways in which the plurality of times relate to each other on the synchronization/desynchronization axis.*

To structure the discussions, we are going to examine two sets of time conflicts. First, we will briefly sketch the time conflicts of modernity as emerging out of efforts to synchronize multiple times in a processual temporality of development, in which some lead the development while others lag behind. These are familiar conflicts intrinsic to modern conceptions of historical time, unveiled by decades of postcolonial and decolonial criticism. Second, and most importantly, we will explore how, in the fabric of historical time, we do not simply witness conflicts within stages of development on a synchronized timeline, but also conflicts of different *kinds* of time and different kinds of out-of-sync temporalities and historicities that inform different domains of life in the human societal endeavor as well as more-than-human temporalities. Whereas the conflicts in the first set are typical of modern historical time (Section 1), the conflicts in the second set characterize the new multiplicity of historical times (Section 2). Conflicts in the fabric of historical time occur in both arrangements of multiple temporalities, as well as between the larger arrangements themselves.

Time Conflicts in Synchronized Time

Conflicts among the plurality of times are intrinsic to modern historical time. As long as attempts are made to synchronize the multiplicity of times into a unitary historical process, the diverging paces, tempos, and rhythms of the sociopolitical world will continue to be seen through a logic that distinguishes between those who lead the development and steer the historical process and those who lag behind and are expected (and often violently forced) to follow the preset course of developments. The previous sections have introduced this constellation of temporal registers with the help of two notions: first, the non-contemporaneity of the contemporaneous (or non-synchronicity of the synchronous), and second, the metaphor of Chakrabarty (2000: 8) concerning the "imaginary waiting room of history" into which those who lag behind are consigned in modern historical time.

The conflicts arising out of modern historical time are not mere abstractions. To a large extent, the non-contemporaneity of the contemporaneous, having been translated into notions of leaders of development and backwardness, served as a tool of legitimation for the Western colonial enterprise, old and new forms of resource extractions (Riofrancos 2017; Lochery 2022), and histories of violence (Ghosh 2021). At the same time, the very same assumptions – the combination of developmental processuality and a synchronized timeline for a unitary historical process – have enabled the sociopolitical struggles of the modern period around emancipation, abolition, and women's suffrage. These assumptions, just like the time conflicts arising out of them, have not disappeared with the waning of modern historical time. Emancipatory projects have been adapted to the realities of the lifeworlds of the new millennium.

As to processuality, we have shown how it constitutes an integral element of the fabric of historical time even in the first decades of the twenty-first century. From the retained forms of progress thinking through emancipatory agendas (which, in principle, can infinitely identify and include new marginalized subjects) to the basic historicist premises of the decolonial imperative (which see the malaises of today as evolving through long-term historical processes driven by past colonial practices), developmental processuality remains the default temporal setting. But what about synchronization efforts on the larger scale? What about the assumption of a unitary historical process?

Despite all skepticism toward universal history in the human and social sciences, the idea has never really ceased to fascinate popular and everyday imagination. Nor has it ceased to constitute one of the most fundamental assumptions of human and social scientific practice. Louis Mink (1987: 194) spoke to the point in the second half of the past century by claiming that "the concept of universal *history* has not been abandoned at all, only the concept of universal *historiography*." Even if not as a history of humanity written by historians and philosophers of history, universal history has survived as the assumption that "everything belongs to a single and determinate realm of unchanging actuality" – that is, the assumption that the past is "an untold story" waiting to be recovered. And even if this idea, as Mink (1987: 194) maintained, "has retreated from the arena of conscious belief and controversy," it is only in order "to habituate itself as a presupposition in that area of our a priori conceptual framework which resists explicit statement and examination." Half a century later, the rise of big history (Hesketh 2023), Anthropocene time, and the demand to see human history at its largest as implicated in Earth System histories, may even pave the way for the emergence of new forms of universal history (in the old sense) and new speculative philosophies of history (cf. Ankersmit 2021).

Nothing testifies more clearly to the survival of universal history, in one form or another, than the continuing existence of time conflicts intrinsic to it, even in discussions around the Anthropocene. True enough, as we have seen, Anthropocene concerns point beyond the scope of modern historical time in many respects and thereby reach beyond the familiar time conflicts of modernity. At the same time, a set of Anthropocene-related time conflicts remains focused on the sociopolitical domain and revolve around the question of being in sync across the globe. Chakrabarty's most recent work is, again, the most attentive to such conflicts. For the "first in Europe, then elsewhere" structure of historical time that Chakrabarty explored in *Provincializing Europe* (2000) is now being adapted to the climate and Anthropocene politics of the day, as examined in *The Climate of History in the Planetary Age* (2021).

At the same time as the West upholds critiques of modernization and begins to see modernization practices as drivers of environmental degradation and planetary crises, there is a "widespread desire for growth, modernization, development, whatever one calls it, in the less developed nations of the world" (Chakrabarty 2021: 96). "The anticolonial desire to modernize," however, "was not simply a repetition of the European modernizer's gesture," as "the global project of modernity got a second and original life in the hands of anticolonial modernizers" (Chakrabarty 2021: 111). Idealistic, spiritual, and ethical, as well as relying on technology and science, "the story of anticolonial, third-world modernizers has to be taken into account" if we want to understand "the depths of the human predicament today" (Chakrabarty 2021: 103).

Yet what happens instead on the modernization front in recent climate and Anthropocene discussions is that past colonial modernizers tend to demand present anticolonial modernizers to follow their lead once again. On this note, and several times throughout his argumentation, Chakrabarty (2021) calls into view the points environmentalists Anil Agarwal and Sunita Narain made more than thirty years ago in a short document entitled *Global Warming in an Unequal World: A Case of Environmental Colonialism* (1991), published by the Centre for Science and Environment in New Delhi. The document is prompted by a joint publication of the World Resources Institute based in the United States and the United Nations, which, Agarwal and Narain (1991: 1) argue, is based on the intention "to blame developing countries for global warming and perpetuate the current global inequality in the use of earth's environment and resources."

The importance of the document in our context, however, lies less with the question of who's to blame for the current planetary crises and more with the temporal aspects and the potential time conflicts emerging from the "fear" in "many developing countries" that "the proposed climate convention will put serious brakes on their development by limiting their ability to produce energy" (Agarwal and Narain 1991: 1). In highlighting and commenting on this passage, Chakrabarty (2021: 160) notes that such an argument for climate justice works "as an argument in world history," as does the title notion of "environmental colonialism" in which "a particular and familiar narrative of European imperialism was encrypted."

We would like to highlight how paradoxical Western expectations to catch up even with the latest anti-modernization impulse and move forward to (technology-driven) sustainable futures share the assumptions of processual time and a synchronized unitary historical process with anticolonial critiques. These assumptions, as long as they survive and get carried over from context to context, harbor familiar time conflicts inherited from modernity.

Conflicts of Desynchronized Temporalities and Historicities

Inasmuch as synchronization efforts fail or the default temporal setting is a multiplicity of desynchronized times, conflicts may take two distinct shapes. First, in cases when the multiple temporalities share a processual character, the time conflicts between processual timelines revolve around the question of pace-setting. Second, inasmuch as not even processuality is shared, desynchronization and conflict concern not multiple temporalities but multiple historicities. Let's take a closer look at both sets of conflicts.

As for conflicts of desynchronized processual temporalities, Hartmut Rosa's theory of social acceleration, mentioned in Section 2, is the perfect guide to an understanding of the conditions of their possibility. As a point of departure, consider how "the function of the political domain in the modern period has been to oversee, supervise and steer" the overall project of human societal betterment (Simon 2019a: 180). What this means in the words of Rosa (2013: 255) is that modernity is characterized by the view that "society is a political project to be shaped within historical time." In late modernity, however, politics is struggling to fulfill this function. Rosa (2013: 259) identifies a "temporal crisis of the political," which consists of "the desynchronization between the 'intrinsic temporality' of politics and the time structures of other social spheres, in particular the economy and technological development, but increasingly also between political organization and sociocultural development." Such desynchronization, in Rosa's theory, takes place against the backdrop of the acceleration of the pace of change in a variety of human endeavors from the sphere of everyday life to the technological domain. Politics, however, cannot keep up with acceleration, and, as "the time horizon and working speed of politics in late modernity lags behind changes in the economy and in society, it can no longer perform the function of setting the pace for social development and being a shaper of history" (Rosa 2013: 267).

This means, in our context, that *time conflicts of social acceleration are conflicts about pace-setting*. As long as the one who sets the pace is tasked with shaping history on the assumption of a unitary historical process, an entailed normative demand of synchronization underpins even conceptions of desynchronized temporalities.[5] This demand applies even to the "countertempos" of modern Egypt, explored by On Barak (2013). The synchronization demand of technology-driven modernization manifested in Egypt most tangibly in the spheres of transportation and communication, from steamers through railroads to telegraphs and telephone. However, instead of simply giving in to the demand of keeping up with the imperative of speeding up, "a new cultural sphere was created, one associated with superstition, slowness, and belatedness, but also with authenticity, religion, and pure Egyptian customs" (Barak 2013: 4). At the same time, none of this resulted in mere antimodern and antitechnological tendencies. According to Barak (2013: 7), "whether discussing the tram's contribution to a dislike for motorized speed, the train's role in the development of elastic standards of colonial punctuality, or the telephone's role in eroticizing delay, Egyptian countertempos emerge as technological and modern."

---

[5] More recently, Rosa (2020) considers the modern relationship to the world in terms of a tension between a desire for control and the inherent uncontrollability of the world (of which new forms are constantly produced precisely by the drive to control – and fail). Seeing this in light of Rosa's earlier work and in the context of this Element would allow an interpretation according to which, in a setting of desynchronized processual temporalities, the time conflicts that revolve around pace-setting arise out of the dialectic of a desire for control and uncontrollability.

As for synchronization, countertempos make clear how much synchronization practices are infused with power. Either in the context of synchronizing times in different domains of human endeavor or in the context of colonialism, synchronization is seldom a practice of reciprocal relations and mutual consent. It is in a web of such power relations that conflicts are intrinsic to the fabric of historical time. The question arising from this constellation is whether it is possible to arrive at more just societal constellations by abandoning the demand of synchronization, together with its containing idea of a universal history. Is there a way to recognize the coexistence of desynchronized historicities? Our final claim is that there most certainly is: desynchronization without a background unitary timeline is not only possible, but it already characterizes twenty-first-century societal practices and discourses to a large extent. However, what the lack of the assumption of a unitary history discloses is not a just arrangement of societal life and human endeavors; it is an entirely different set of conflicts.

A genuine abandonment of the assumption of a universal history reveals not multiple temporalities but multiple historicities. The conflicts intrinsic to such multiple historicities concern not pace-setting but *coexisting imaginaries, discourses, and practices that either implicitly entail or explicitly invoke competing conceptions of change over time.* These are conflicts about what makes a desired future and about the kinds of transition from apprehended pasts to such futures – that is, conflicts of what we have discussed as modalities of "historical futures" (Simon and Tamm 2021). Whereas time conflicts of acceleration represent conflicts internal to a processual temporality, the conflicts of desynchronized historicities see all processual scenarios of change over time in one bloc and in relation to other kinds of transitional configurations. To get a better grasp on the difference, consider the desynchronization of politics noted by Rosa as a desynchronization of historicities. Seen in terms of conflicting historicities rather than conflicting temporalities, when "the crisis of the political is rather the result of a change in the perception of the temporal configuration of change other than the political, and the new configuration poses an external challenge to the entire processual historical sensibility, then the crisis lies in the divergence of kinds of change" (Simon 2019a: 193).

Conflicts of desynchronized historicities, we believe, characterize twenty-first-century societies at the most profound level. Without aiming at a complete overview of extremely large complexities, we intend to offer an insight into such conflicts by briefly zooming in on two examples. The first example consists of the conflicts between the desynchronized historicities of technological and political change, while the second one highlights desynchronized historicities at play within the political domain, in conflicts arising out of diverging conceptions of and relations to historical injustice.

To begin with conflicts around technological change, perhaps it amounts to a truism by now to state that the perceived capacities of technology gained a new quality around the middle of the past century. Hannah Arendt (1961: 58), a contemporary observer and interpreter, distinguished her own age from the modern age and argued that human development had reached a new stage when "we have begun to act into nature as we used to act into history." Another contemporary, Julian Huxley (1968 [1957]), usually considered the founding figure of transhumanism, went even further in explicitly advocating such ways of acting into nature with the help of advanced technologies, "as if man had been suddenly appointed managing director of the biggest business of all, the business of evolution."

Although in the middle of the century both Huxley and Arendt kept on thinking about change in terms of developmental processes, the tide had changed by the end of century. Prospects of technological capacities had increasingly tended toward anticipations of technological singularity scenarios and runaway changes through the creation of greater-than-human intelligence, as reviewed in Section 2. Should the singularity happen, it is expected to be "a throwing away of all the previous rules, perhaps in the blink of an eye," and "a point where our models must be discarded and a new reality rules" (Vinge 1993). The fact that the singularity has not happened, the possibility that it never will, or the humanistic interpretations of predictive tech, emphasizing that such technologies try to convince about their potential by ritualized demonstrations rather than reality-altering innovations (Hong 2022), do not diminish the significance of the prospects and aims of technology actors to transition into futures in ways other than conventional historical processes.

As we have learned from Rosa's theory, the political domain finds itself today in a reactionary relation to technological change. Yet such political reactions may point beyond the frame of the theory of social acceleration and its focus on pace-setting in several aspects. To begin with, the relations vary in regard to the kind of politics one pursues. Institutions and actors of nation-state and international politics, as well as resourceful research institutions, tend to focus on large-scale policy agendas aimed at containing and confining technological capacities. Nowhere is the goal of containment more tangible than in the politics of AI alignment, which, as its name suggests, intends "to ensure that powerful AI is properly aligned with human values" (Gabriel 2020: 412). The inherent paradox of the politics of AI alignment is, of course, the fact that ultimately it effaces the "artificial" in "artificial intelligence" by making sure that it remains "human." In that, it works against and necessarily conflicts with any ambition directed toward the creation of greater-than-human intelligence, which, by definition, was supposed go beyond what is conceived of as human.

As a conflict of historicities, AI alignment is premised on ensuring the continuing reign of a conception of history we know from Western modernity, a cumulative progress of the human world, set against a conception of history that entails noncumulative and nonprocessual transitions into a more-than-human world. This, however, is not the only conflict between the desynchronized historicities of political and technological change. For an entirely different kind of politics, the politics of social justice, conflicts with technological capacities and conceptions of technological change on another level, much closer to the experienced realities of everyday life. In confronting the social harms of technology, it brings to light the many ways in which algorithms discriminate and reinforce existing inequalities and create new ones (Noble 2018; Benjamin 2019), and it unveils the costs of human labor and the environmental costs behind the showcased advancements in AI (Gray and Suri 2019; Crawford 2021). In doing so, it makes visible yet another conflict between runaway technological and processual political and social change, in which the latter remain committed to emancipatory conceptions of modern history.

Even though emancipatory politics and the politics of AI alignment may indeed rely on historicities inherited from the modern world, this does not mean that the political domain as such would entail one historicity. In its relation to other domains, it is, of course, possible and important to see the political domain *en bloc*, but this should not prevent us from recognizing that political change itself is subject to a conflict of historicities. The multiple historicities surveyed in Section 2 can, in principle, enter conflictual relations with each other in various ways. In fact, some temporalities are also prone to being reconceived as historicities inasmuch as they entail transitional relations. For instance, the time of the imprescriptible and the politics of historical injustice debates can turn time conflicts into conflicts of historicities, as we think happened in the case of the debates around the Rhodes Must Fall protests at universities in South Africa. Even though Fareld (2019) approaches the protests and the removal of statues of Rhodes as time conflicts, it seems to us that the conflict between the views of protestors and the views of historians voicing concerns about "the growing intermingling of history and justice" – as Fareld phrases it (2019: 59) – is rather a conflict of historicities about social and political change. The persistence and the presence of the past in the present in historical injustice, on the one hand, and the codes of disciplinary history writing to posit a temporal distance to what it subjects to historical study, on the other, represent "opposing ideas about the very transition between past and present" (Fareld 2019: 65).

Rather than being time conflicts about pace-setting, the conflicts of historicities manifest here in diverging present relations to the past. Professional historiography's insistence on histories of developmental processes that, over time, gradually fade out the imprint of the past on the present is at odds with the protesters' experience of the full weight of the past burdening the present not only in the shape of surviving colonial statues and political decolonization but also in regard to the survival of epistemic colonization. And the latter even points to another level of conflict of historicities, which highlights the future and the prospect of transitions. For according to the analysis of Sabelo J. Ndlovu-Gatsheni (2018: 239), what "we are witnessing is rapture, not simply from transformation to decolonization but from the idea of South Africa to the South African idea, this time defined and shaped by descendants of the enslaved, colonized, racialized, dispossessed and dehumanized." What protesters "are loudly proclaiming" is "that their lives matter and they were born into valid and legitimate knowledge systems that have been pushed out of the academy" (Ndlovu-Gatsheni 2018: 239).

All in all, we believe that maintaining a distinction between time conflicts and conflicts of historicities can be a crucial step toward developing a better understanding of the nature of history-infused conflicts in our societies. Such an understanding constitutes the basis of being able to attend these conflicts without failing to recognize their complexities.

One Fabric, Many Times: A Resolution

The fabric of historical time consists of varying relational arrangements and interactions of multiple temporalities and historicities. Kinds of temporalities and historicities emerge, come to being, fade out, transform, cease to exist, merge, coexist, overlap, arrange and rearrange in constellations of the temporal registers (of past, present, and future), clash, and conflict in a dynamic without a predetermined plot. We have attempted to testify to this dynamic by sketching modern arrangements and constellations as well as contemporary ones, indicating transformations in the fabric of historical time while at the same time being aware of the ephemeral nature of the whole endeavor. One might nevertheless ask whether the multiplicity we have recounted and the transience we have hinted at in the previous pages are at odds with the metaphor of one singular fabric. Our response would be that there is no contradiction at all. In fact, we think that the greatest benefit of the fabric metaphor is precisely that it enables us to consistently talk about *one* fabric and *many* temporalities and historicities inasmuch as that fabric is seen as relational, elastic, and dynamic – inasmuch as the fabric itself is seen as historical.

Our "one fabric, many times" approach brings a resolution to the conundrum Chris Lorenz fleshed out in a discussion in Bochum about Ethan Kleinberg's Koselleck Lecture of 2021. The title of Lorenz's comment, "Taking Plural Times Seriously," perfectly conveys its central message. Recall Section 2, where we quoted the perhaps strictest sentence of the comment, claiming that "in a pluriform temporal universe *no one* – including historical theorists – is allowed to claim anything by just referring to '*the*' past, '*the*' present and '*the*' future, because 'the' past, present and future *only exist in the plural*." Here, we would like to quote Lorenz (2021) a bit more extensively, putting this sentence in the larger context of the comment and thereby bringing out more prominently the stakes of the claim:

> [T]aking plural times seriously implies first and foremost that uniform and "exclusive" temporal labels are strictly banned. In a pluriform temporal universe *no one* – including historical theorists – is allowed to claim anything by just referring to "*the*" past, "*the*" present and "*the*" future, because "the" past, present and future *only exist in the plural*. Neither is anyone – including historical theorists – allowed to invoke "*our* past," "*our* present" and "*our* future" as an argument for a specific periodization because there is no uniform "we." Therefore I think that advocates of pluralism in the domain of time should be very careful with both the use of definite articles ("the") and the use of possessive pronouns ("our") when they propose a period-label . . . In sum: when a historical theorist throws out uniform time through the front door . . . it is a matter of consistency *not* to reintroduce uniform time through the backdoor of uniform period labels.

Taking plural times seriously is a difficult job. As Lorenz (2021) is perfectly aware, "old habits usually die hard, and this rule applies to thinking about historical time too." And even if one succeeds in consistently making the case for historical times in the plural, it does not even mean completely abandoning the developmental processuality of modern Western conceptions of historical time. For one, as we have seen, modern historical time was already conceived of as consisting of many times. And, as we have also seen, modernist conceptions survive today in many shapes across a broad spectrum of political views: from the continuing necessity of emancipatory politics through economic policies to transhumanist self-branding. The difficulty of taking plural times seriously lies, on the one hand, with recognizing both the practical survival of modernist conceptions and their confines, especially by societal practices that continue to rely on them, be such practices colonial or decolonial (or neither or both). On the other hand, it lies with recognizing other-than-modernist temporalities and historicities without projecting modernist conceptions over them, without "timelining" them, as Shahzad Bashir (2022) would have it.

Avoiding the reintroduction of the uniformity (and the synchronization) demand intrinsic to modern conceptions of historical time does not work by thinking that one conception of time and history can simply replace another one. It works only by recognizing that these conceptions coexist in a web of ever-changing relational arrangements of complex interactions. This web is what we call the fabric of historical time.

References

Agarwal, Anil, and Sunita Narain (1991). *Global Warming in an Unequal World: A Case of Environmental Colonialism*. New Delhi: Centre for Science and Environment.

Althusser, Louis, and Étienne Balibar (1970). *Reading "Capital"*. Trans. Ben Brewster. London: New Left Books.

Ankersmit, Frank (2006). "Presence" and Myth. *History and Theory* 45(3): 328–336.

Ankersmit, Frank (2021). The Thorn of History: Unintended Consequences and Speculative Philosophy of History. *History and Theory* 60(2): 187–214.

Arendt, Hannah (1961). The Concept of History: Ancient and Modern. In Hannah Arendt, *Between Past and Future: Six Exercises in Political Thought*. New York: Viking Press, 41–90.

Assmann, Aleida (2020). *Is Time Out of Joint? On the Rise and Fall of the Modern Time Regime*. Trans. Sarah Clift. Ithaca, NY: Cornell University Press.

Assmann, Jan (1997). *Moses the Egyptian: The Memory of Egypt in Western Monotheism*. Cambridge, MA: Harvard University Press.

Azhar, Azeem (2021). *Exponential: How Accelerating Technology Is Leaving Us behind and What to Do about It*. London: Random House Business.

Banerjee, Prathama (2006). *Politics of Time: "Primitives" and History-Writing in a Colonial Society*. New Delhi: Oxford University Press.

Bantigny, Ludivine (2013). Historicités du 20e siècle: Quelques jalons sur une notion. *Vingtième Siècle: Revue d'histoire* 117: 13–25.

Barak, On (2013). *On Time: Technology and Temporality in Modern Egypt*. Berkeley: University of California Press.

Barkan, Elazar (2009). Introduction: Historians and Historical Reconciliation. *American Historical Review* 114(4): 899–913.

Baschet, Jérôme (2018). *Défaire la tyrannie du présent: Temporalités émergentes et futurs inédits*. Paris: La Découverte.

Baschet, Jérôme (2021). *Basculements: Mondes émergents, possibles désirables*. Paris: La Découverte.

Baschet, Jérôme (2022). Reopening the Future: Emerging Worlds and Novel Historical Futures. *History and Theory* 61(2): 183–208.

Bashir, Shahzad (2022). *A New Vision for Islamic Pasts and Futures*. Cambridge, MA: MIT Press. https://islamic-pasts-futures.org.

Benjamin, Ruha (2019). *Race after Technology: Abolitionist Tools for the New Jim Code*. Cambridge: Polity.

Berger, Stefan (2022). *History and Identity: How Historical Theory Shapes Historical Practice*. Cambridge: Cambridge University Press.

Bergwik, Staffan, and Anders Ekström (2022). Introduction: Dividing Times. In Anders Ekström and Staffan Bergwik, eds., *Times of History, Times of Nature: Temporalization and the Limits of Modern Knowledge*. New York: Berghahn, 1–16.

Bevernage, Berber (2008). Time, Presence, and Historical Injustice. *History and Theory* 47(2): 149–167.

Bevernage, Berber (2011). *History, Memory, and State-Sponsored Violence: Time and Justice*. New York: Routledge.

Bevernage, Berber (2016). Tales of Pastness and Contemporaneity: On the Politics of Time in History and Anthropology. *Rethinking History* 20(3): 352–374.

Bevernage, Berber, and Chris Lorenz (2013). Breaking Up Time: Negotiating the Borders between Present, Past, and Future. *Storia della Storiografia* 63: 31–50.

Bloch, Ernst (1985). *Erbschaft dieser Zeit. Werkausgabe*, vol. 4. Frankfurt: Suhrkamp.

Bodei, Remo (1979). *Multiversum: Tempo e storia in Ernst Bloch*. Naples: Bibliopolis.

Bonaldo, Rodrigo, and Ana Carolina Barbosa Pereira (2023). Potential History: Reading Artificial Intelligence from Indigenous Knowledges. *History and Theory* 62(1): 3–29.

Bonneuil, Christophe (2020). Der Historiker und der Planet: Planetaritätsregimes an der Schnittstelle von Welt-Ökologien, ökologischen Reflexivitäten und Geo-Mächten. In Frank Adloff and Sighard Neckel, eds., *Gesellschaftstheorie im Anthropozän*. Frankfurt: Campus, 55–92.

Bos, Jacques (2021). Presence. In Chiel van den Akker, ed., *The Routledge Companion to Historical Theory*. London: Routledge, 573–586.

Bouton, Christophe (2018). Dealing with Deep Time: The Issue of Ancestrality from Kant to Hegel. *Res: Anthropology and Aesthetics* 69–70: 38–51.

Bouton, Christophe (2022). *L'Accélération de l'histoire: Des Lumières à l'Anthropocène*. Paris: Seuil.

Braidotti, Rosi (2013). *The Posthuman*. Cambridge: Polity.

Braidotti, Rosi (2019). *The Posthuman Knowledge*. Cambridge: Polity.

Braudel, Fernand (1958). Histoire et sciences sociales: La longue durée. *Annales: Économies, Sociétés, Civilisations* 13(4): 725–753.

Bray, Tamara L. (2018). Archaeology, Temporal Complexity, and the Politics of Time. In Edward Swenson and Andrew Roddick, eds., *Constructions of Time and History in the Pre-Columbian Andes*. Boulder: University Press of Colorado, 263–278.

Browne, Victoria (2014). *Feminism, Time, and Nonlinear History: A Polytemporal Approach*. New York: Palgrave.

Burke, Peter (2011). Exemplarity and Anti-exemplarity in Early Modern Europe. In Alexandra Lianeri, ed., *The Western Time of Ancient History: Historiographical Encounters with the Greek and Roman Pasts*. Cambridge: Cambridge University Press, 48–59.

Castells, Manuel (1996). *The Rise of the Network Society*. Oxford: Blackwell.

Chakrabarty, Dipesh (2000). *Provincializing Europe: Postcolonial Thought and Historical Difference*. Princeton, NJ: Princeton University Press.

Chakrabarty, Dipesh (2021). *The Climate of History in a Planetary Age*. Chicago, IL: University of Chicago Press.

Connell, Raewyn (2018). Decolonizing Sociology. *Contemporary Sociology: A Journal of Reviews* 47(4): 399–407.

Conrad, Sebastian (2018). "Nothing Is the Way It Should Be": Global Transformations of the Time Regime in the Nineteenth Century. *Modern Intellectual History* 15(3), 821–848.

Coole, Diana, and Samantha Frost, ed. (2010). *New Materialisms: Ontology, Agency, and Politics*. Durham, NC: Duke University Press.

Cooper, Anwen, Duncan Garrow, Catriona Gibson, Melanie Giles, and Neil Wilkin (2022). *Grave Goods: Objects and Death in Later Prehistoric Britain*. Oxford: Oxbow Books.

Crawford, Kate (2021). *Atlas of AI: Power, Politics, and the Planetary Costs of Artificial Intelligence*. New Haven, CT: Yale University Press.

Crist, Eileen, and Helen Kopnina (2014). Unsettling Anthropocentrism. *Dialectical Anthropology* 38(4): 387–396.

Davis, Heather, and Zoe Todd (2017). On the Importance of a Date, or Decolonizing the Anthropocene. *ACME: An International Journal for Critical Geographies* 16(4): 761–780.

Davis, Kathleen (2008). *Periodization and Sovereignty: How Ideas of Feudalism and Secularization Govern the Politics of Time*. Philadelphia: University of Pennsylvania Press.

De Baets, Antoon (2011). Historical Imprescriptibility. *Storia della Storiografia* 59–60: 128–149.

Décultot, Elizabeth, and Daniel Fulda, eds. (2016). *Sattelzeit: Historiographiegeschichtliche Revisionen*. Berlin: De Gruyter.

Derrida, Jacques (2006). *Specters of Marx: The State of the Debt, the Work of Mourning, and the New International*. Trans. Peggy Kamuf. New York: Routledge.

Deutsch, David (1998). *The Fabric of Reality: The Science of Parallel Universes – and Its Implications*. New York: Penguin.

Devun, Leah, and Zeb Tortorici (2018). Trans, Time, and History. *TSQ: Transgender Studies Quarterly* 5(4): 518–539.

Didi-Huberman, Georges (2002). *L'image survivante: Histoire de l'art et temps des fantômes selon Aby Warburg*. Paris: Minuit.

Dodd, Nigel, and Judy Wajcman (2017). Simmel and Benjamin: Early Theorists of the Acceleration Society. In Judy Wajcman and Nigel Dodd, eds., *The Sociology of Speed: Digital, Organizational, and Social Temporalities*. Oxford: Oxford University Press, 13–24.

Domanska, Ewa (2010). Beyond Anthropocentrism in Historical Studies. *Historein* 10: 118–130.

Dube, Saurabh, and Ishita Banerjee-Dube, eds. (2006). *Unbecoming Modern: Colonialism, Modernity, Colonial Modernities*. New Delhi: Social Science Press.

Dürbeck, Gabriele, and Philip Hüpkes, eds. (2022). *Narratives of Scale in the Anthropocene: Imagining Human Responsibility in an Age of Scalar Complexity*. London: Routledge.

Edelstein, Dan, Stefanos Geroulanos, and Natasha Wheatley, eds. (2020a). *Power and Time: Temporalities in Conflict and the Making of History*. Chicago, IL: University of Chicago Press.

Edelstein, Dan, Stefanos Geroulanos, and Natasha Wheatley (2020b). Chronocenosis: An Introduction to Power and Time. In Dan Edelstein, Stefanos Geroulanos, and Natasha Wheatley, eds., *Power and Time: Temporalities in Conflict and the Making of History*. Chicago, IL: University of Chicago Press, 1–49.

Ekström, Anders, and Staffan Bergwik, eds. (2022). *Times of History, Times of Nature: Temporalization and the Limits of Modern Knowledge*. New York: Berghahn.

Esposito, Fernando, ed. (2017). *Zeitenwandel: Transformationen geschichtlicher Zeitlichkeit nach dem Boom*. Gottingen: Vandenhoek & Ruprecht.

Fareld, Victoria (2018). History, Justice and the Time of the Imprescriptible. In Stefan Helgesson and Jayne Svenungsson, eds., *The Ethos of History: Time and Responsibility*. New York: Berghahn, 54–69.

Fareld, Victoria (2019). Coming to Terms with the Present: Exploring the Chrononormativity of Historical Time. In Marek Tamm and Laurent Olivier, eds., *Rethinking Historical Time: New Approaches to Presentism*. London: Bloomsbury Academic, 57–70.

Fareld, Vitoria (2022a) Time. In Chiel van den Akker, ed., *The Routledge Companion to Historical Theory*. London: Routledge, 558–572.

Fareld, Victora (2022b). Framing the Polychronic Present. In Zoltán Boldizsár Simon and Lars Deile, eds., *Historical Understanding: Past, Present, and Future*. London: Bloomsbury Academic, 25–33.

Fernández-Sebastian, Javier (2016). A World in the Making: Discovering the Future in the Hispanic World. *Contributions to the History of Concepts* 11 (2): 110–132.

Ferrando, Francesca (2019). *Philosophical Posthumanism*. London: Bloomsbury Academic.

Friedman, Susan Stanford (2019). Alternatives to Periodization: Literary History, Modernism, and the "New" Temporalities. *Modern Language Quarterly* 80(4): 379–402.

Frieman, Catherine J. (2023). *Archaeology As History: Telling Stories from a Fragmented Past*. Cambridge: Cambridge University Press.

Fryxell, Allegra F. P. (2019). Time and the Modern: Current Trends in the History of Modern Temporalities. *Past and Present* 243: 285–298.

Fuchs, Anne (2019). *Precarious Times: Temporality and History in Modern German Culture*. Ithaca, NY: Cornell University Press.

Fuchs, Anne (2022). Chronic Crisis Novels and the Quest for "the Good-Enough Life": Kathrin Röggla's *Die Alarmbereiten*, Kristine Bilkau's *Die Glücklichen*, and Thorsten Nagelschmidt's *Arbeit*. *Seminar: A Journal of Germanic Studies* 58(3): 328–348.

Gabriel, Iason (2020). Artificial Intelligence, Values, and Alignment. *Minds and Machines* 30: 411–437.

González-Ruibal, Alfredo (2006). The Past Is Tomorrow: Towards an Archaeology of the Vanishing Present. *Norwegian Archaeological Review* 39(2): 110–125.

González-Ruibal, Alfredo (2016). Archaeology and the Time of Modernity. *Historical Archaeology* 50(3): 144–164.

Ghosh, Amitav (2021). *The Nutmeg's Curse: Parables for a Planet in Crisis*. Chicago, IL: University of Chicago Press.

Ghosh, Ranjan, and Ethan Kleinberg, eds. (2013). *Presence: Philosophy, History, and Cultural Theory for the Twenty-First Century*. Ithaca, NY: Cornell University Press.

Gould, Stephen Jay (1987). *Time's Arrow, Time's Cycle: Myth and Metaphor in the Discovery of Geological Time*. Cambridge, MA: Harvard University Press.

Grave, Johannes (2019). Pictorial Temporality and the Times of History: On Seeing Images and Experiencing Time. In Marek Tamm and Laurent Olivier, eds., *Rethinking Historical Time: New Approaches to Presentism*. London: Bloomsbury Academic, 117–130.

Gray, Mary L., and Siddharth Suri (2019). *Ghost Work: How to Stop Silicon Valley from Building a New Global Underclass*. Boston, MA: Houghton Mifflin Harcourt.

Greene, Brian (2004). *The Fabric of the Cosmos: Space, Time, and the Texture of Reality*. New York: Alfred A. Knopf.

Grinspoon, David (2016). *Earth in Human Hands: Shaping Our Planet's Future*. New York: Grand Central.

Grosfoguel, Ramón (2000). Developmentalism, Modernity, and Dependency Theory in Latin America. *Nepantla: Views from South* 1(2): 347–374.

Guha, Ranajit (2002). *History at the Limit of World-History*. New York: Columbia University Press.

Gumbrecht, Hans Ulrich (2004). *Production of Presence: What Meaning Cannot Convey*. Stanford, CA: Stanford University Press.

Gumbrecht, Hans Ulrich (2014). *Our Broad Present: Time and Contemporary Culture*. New York: Columbia University Press.

Gurvitch, Georges (1958). *La multiplicité des temps sociaux*. Paris: Centre de documentation universitaire.

Gurvitch, Georges (1964). *The Spectrum of Social Time*. Trans. Myrtle Korenbaum. Dordrecht: Reidel.

Halbwachs, Maurice (1950). *La mémoire collective*. Paris: Presses Universitaires de France.

Hamann, Byron Ellsworth (2016). How to Chronologize with a Hammer, Or, The Myth of Homogeneous, Empty Time. *Hau: Journal of Ethnographic Theory* 6(1): 261–292.

Haraway, Donna J. (2016). *Staying with the Trouble: Making Kin in the Chthulucene*. Durham, NC: Duke University Press.

Harmanşah, Ömür (2020). Deep Time and Landscape History: How Can Historical Particularity Be Translated? In Bethany Wiggin, Carolyn Fornoff, and Patricia Eunji Kim, eds., *Timescales: Thinking across Ecological Temporalities*. Minneapolis: University of Minnesota Press, 39–53.

Harootunian, Harry (2015). *Marx after Marx: History and Time in the Expansion of Capitalism*. New York: Columbia University Press.

Harris, Olivia (2004). Braudel: Historical Time and the Horror of Discontinuity. *History Workshop Journal* 57(1): 161–174.

Hartog, François (2015). *Regimes of Historicity: Presentism and Experiences of Time*. Trans. Saskia Brown. New York: Columbia University Press.

Hartog, François (2022). *Chronos: The West Confronts Time*. Trans. Sam Gilbert. New York: Columbia University Press.

Hassan, Robert (2009). *Empires of Speed: Time and the Acceleration of Politics and Society*. Leiden: Brill.

Helgesson, Stefan (2014). Radicalizing Temporal Difference: Anthropology, Postcolonial Theory, and Literary Time. *History and Theory* 53(4): 545–562.

Hellerma, Juhan (2020). Koselleck on Modernity, *Historik*, and Layers of Time. *History and Theory* 59(2): 188–209.

Hellerma, Juhan (2021). History on the Move: Reimagining Historical Change and the (Im)Possibility of Utopia in the 21st Century. *Journal of the Philosophy of History* 15(2): 249–262.

Henry, Charles P. (2003). The Politics of Racial Reparations. *Journal of Black Studies* 34(2): 131–152.

Herder, Johann Gottfried (1998). "Eine Metakritik zur Kritik der reinen Vernunft," in *Schriften zur Literatur und Philosophie 1792–1800*. Berlin: Deutscher Klassiker.

Hesketh, Ian (2023). *A History of Big History*. Cambridge: Cambridge University Press.

Hirsch, Eric, and Charles Stewart (2005). Introduction: Ethnographies of Historicity. *History and Anthropology* 16(3): 261–274.

Hochkirchen, Britta (2021). Beyond Representation: Pictorial Temporality and the Relational Time of the Event. *History and Theory* 60(1): 102–116.

Hölscher, Lucian (2016). *Die Entdeckung der Zukunft*. Gottingen: Wallstein.

Hölscher, Lucian (2020). *Zeitgärten. Zeitfiguren in der Geschichte der Neuzeit*. Gottingen: Wallstein.

Hong, Sun-ha (2022). Predictions without Futures. *History and Theory* 61(3): 371–390.

Horn, Eva, and Hannes Bergthaller (2019). *The Anthropocene: Key Issues for the Humanities*. London: Routledge.

Huxley, Julian (1968 [1957]). Transhumanism. *Journal of Humanistic Psychology* 8(1): 73–76.

Iheka, Cajetan (2021). *African Ecomedia: Network Forms, Planetary Politics*. Durham, NC: Duke University Press.

Inoue, Cristina Yumie Aoki (2018). Worlding the Study of Global Environmental Politics in the Anthropocene: Indigenous Voices from the Amazon. *Global Environmental Politics* 18(4): 25–42.

Irvine, Richard D. G. (2020). *An Anthropology of Deep Time: Geological Temporality and Social Life*. Cambridge: Cambridge University Press.

Jordheim, Helge (2014). Introduction: Multiple Times and the Work of Synchronization. *History and Theory* 53(4): 498–518.

Jordheim, Helge (2022a). In Sync/Out of Sync. In Zoltán Boldizsár Simon and Lars Deile, eds., *Historical Understanding: Past, Present, and Future*. London: Bloomsbury Academic, 45–56.

Jordheim, Helge (2022b). Mending Shattered Time: 22 July in Norwegian Collective Memory. In Torgeir Rinke Bangstad and Þóra Pétursdóttir, eds., *Heritage Ecologies*. London: Routledge, 185–207.

Jordheim, Helge (2022c). Natural Histories for the Anthropocene: Koselleck's Theories and the Possibility of a History of Lifetimes. *History and Theory* 61(3): 391–425.

Jordheim, Helge, and Einar Wigen (2018). Conceptual Synchronisation: From Progress to Crisis. *Millennium: Journal of International Studies* 46(3): 421–439.

Jordheim, Helge, and Espen Ytreberg (2021). After Supersynchronisation: How Media Synchronise the Social. *Time & Society* 30(3): 402–422.

Jørgensen, Dolly (2022). Extinction and the End of Futures. *History and Theory* 61(2): 209–218.

Jung, Theo (2010/11). Das Neue der Neuzeit ist ihre Zeit: Reinhart Kosellecks Theorie der Verzeitlichung und ihre Kritiker. *Moderne: Kulturwissenschaftliches Jahrbuch* 6: 172–184.

Karlholm, Dan (2018). Is History to Be Closed, Saved, or Restarted? Considering Efficient Art History. In Dan Karlholm and Keith Moxey, eds., *Time in the History of Art: Temporality, Chronology, and Anachrony*. London: Routledge, 13–25.

Kashwan, Prakash, Frank Biermann, Aarti Gupta, and Chukwumerije Okereke (2020). Planetary Justice: Prioritizing the Poor in Earth System Governance. *Earth System Governance* 6: 100075.

Kleinberg, Ethan (2013). Prologue. In Ranjan Ghosh and Ethan Kleinberg, eds., *Presence: Philosophy, History, and Cultural Theory for the Twenty-First Century*. Ithaca, NY: Cornell University Press, 1–7.

Kleinberg, Ethan (2017). *Haunting History: For a Deconstructive Approach to the Past*. Stanford, CA: Stanford University Press.

Koselleck, Reinhart (1967). *Preussen zwischen Reform und Revolution*. Stuttgart: Ernst Klett Verlag.

Koselleck, Reinhart (2000). *Zeitschichten: Studien zur Historik*. Frankfurt: Suhrkamp.

Koselleck, Reinhart (2004). *Futures Past: On the Semantics of Historical Time*. Trans. Keith Tribe. New York: Columbia University Press.

Koselleck, Reinhart (2018). *Sediments of Time. On Possible Histories*. Trans. and ed. Sean Franzel and Stefan-Ludwig Hoffmann. Stanford, CA: Stanford University Press.

Kurzweil, Ray (2004). The Law of Accelerating Returns. In Christof Teuscher, ed., *Alan Turing: Life and Legacy of a Great Thinker*. Berlin: Springer, 381–416.

Kurzweil, Ray (2005). *The Singularity Is Near: When Humans Transcend Biology*. New York: Viking.

Kverndokk, Kyrre, Marit Ruge Bjærke, and Anne Eriksen, eds. (2021). *Climate Change Temporalities: Explorations in Vernacular, Popular, and Scientific Discourse*. London: Routledge.

Kyung-Sup, Chang (2022). *The Logic of Compressed Modernity*. Cambridge: Polity.

Laki, László (2021). *A "Színlelt" Szocializmusból, A "színlelt" Kapitalizmusba*. Edited by Zoltán Békés. Szeged: Belvedere Meridionale.

Landwehr, Achim, ed. (2012). *Frühe Neuen Zeiten: Zeitwissen zwischen Reformation und Revolution*. Bielefeld: transcript.

Landwehr, Achim (2016). *Die anwesende Abwesenheit der Vergangenheit. Essay zur Geschichtstheorie*. Frankfurt: Fischer.

Landwehr, Achim (2018). Nostalgia and the Turbulence of Times. *History and Theory* 57(2): 251–268.

Landwehr, Achim (2020). *Diesseits der Geschichte: Für eine andere Historiographie*. Gottingen: Wallstein.

Lenton, Timothy M., Hermann Held, Elmar Kriegler et al. (2008). Tipping Elements in the Earth's Climate System. *PNAS* 105(6): 1786–1793.

Lenton, Timothy M., Johan Rockström, Owen Gaffnex et al. (2019). Climate Tipping Points – Too Risky to Bet Against. *Nature* 575: 592–595.

Lianeri, Alexandra, ed. (2011). *The Western Time of Ancient History: Historiographical Encounters with the Greek and Roman Pasts*. Cambridge: Cambridge University Press.

Livingston, Julie (2019). *Self-Devouring Growth: A Planetary Parable As Told from South Africa*. Durham, NC: Duke University Press.

Locher, Fabien, and Jean-Baptiste Fressoz (2012). Modernity's Frail Climate: A Climate History of Environmental Reflexivity. *Critical Inquiry* 38(3): 579–598.

Lochery, Emma (2022). Situating Extraction in Capitalism: Blueprints, Frontier Projects, and Life-Making. *Extractive Industries and Society* 11: 101–137.

Lorenz, Chris (2010). Unstuck in Time. Or: The Sudden Presence of the Past. In Karin Tilmans, Frank van Vree, and Jay Winter, eds., *Performing the Past: Memory, History, and Identity in Modern Europe*. Amsterdam: Amsterdam University Press, 67–102.

Lorenz, Chris (2017). "The Times They Are a-Changin": On Time, Space and Periodization in History. In Mario Carretero, Stefan Berger, and Maria Grever, eds., *Palgrave Handbook of Research in Culture and Education*. London: Palgrave, 109–131.

Lorenz, Chris (2019). Out of Time? Some Critical Reflections on François Hartog's Presentism. In Marek Tamm and Laurent Olivier, eds., *Rethinking Historical Time: New Perspectives on Presentism*. London: Bloomsbury Academic, 23–42.

Lorenz, Chris (2021). Taking Plural Times Seriously: Comments on Ethan Kleinberg's Koselleck lecture (Unpublished paper presented at the Institut für soziale Bewegungen, Bochum, December 14, 2021).

Lorenz, Chris (2022). Probing the Limits of a Metaphor: On the Stratigraphic Model in History and Geology. In Zoltán Boldizsár Simon and Lars Deile, eds., *Historical Understanding: Past, Present, and Future*. London: Bloomsbury Academic, 203–215.

Lotman, Juri (2009). *Culture and Explosion*. Trans. Wilma Clark. Berlin: Mouton de Gruyter.

Lotman, Juri (2019). *Culture, Memory and History: Essays in Cultural Semiotics*. Edited by Marek Tamm, trans. Brian James Baer. London: Palgrave Macmillan.

MacCormack, Patricia (2012). *Posthuman Ethics: Embodiment and Cultural Theory*. Farnham: Ashgate.

Maffesoli, Michel (2003). *L'instant éternel*. Paris: La Table Ronde.

Marx, Karl (1972). *The Eighteenth Brumaire of Louis Bonaparte*. Moscow: Progress.

McEwan, Cheryl (2021). Decolonizing the Anthropocene. In David Chandler, Franziska Müller, and Delf Rothe, eds., *International Relations in the Anthropocene: New Agendas, New Agencies and New Approaches*. Cham: Palgrave, 77–94.

McPhee, John (1981). *Basin and Range*. New York: Farrar, Straus and Giroux.

Meghji, Ali (2021). *Decolonizing Sociology: An Introduction*. Cambridge: Polity.

Mendieta, Eduardo (2020). Anthropocenic Temporalities: The Time of the End and the End of Time. *Environmental Philosophy* 17(1): 125–141.

Merchant, Carolyn (1980). *The Death of Nature: Women, Ecology, and the Scientific Revolution*. San Francisco, CA: Harper & Row.

Merchant, Carolyn (2020). *The Anthropocene and the Humanities: From Climate Change to a New Age of Sustainability*. New Haven, CT: Yale University Press.

Mignolo, Walter D. (2011). *The Darker Side of Western Modernity: Global Futures, Decolonial Options*. Durham, NC: Duke University Press.

Mills, Charles W. (2020). The Chronopolitics of Racial Time. *Time & Society* 29 (2): 297–317.

Mink, L. O. (1987). *Historical Understanding*. Edited by Brian Fay, Eugene O. Golob, and Richard T. Vann. Ithaca, NY: Cornell University Press.

Moore, Jason W., ed. (2016). *Anthropocene or Capitalocene? Nature, History, and the Crisis of Capitalism*. Oakland, CA: Kairos.

More, Max, and Natasha Vita-More, eds. (2013). *The Transhumanist Reader: Classical and Contemporary Essays on the Science, Technology, and Philosophy of the Human Future*. Malden, MA: Wiley-Blackwell.

Morfino, Vittorio (2018). On Non-contemporaneity: Marx, Bloch, Althusser. In Vittorio Morfino and Peter D. Thomas, eds., *The Government of Time: Theories of Plural Temporality in the Marxist Tradition*. Leiden: Brill, 117–147.

Morfino, Vittorio, and Peter D. Thomas (2018). Introduction: *Tempora multa*. In Vittorio Morfino and Peter D. Thomas, eds., *The Government of Time: Theories of Plural Temporality in the Marxist Tradition*. Leiden: Brill, 1–19.

Mudrovcic, María Inés (2021). Regimes of Historicity. In *Bloomsbury History: Theory and Method*. London: Bloomsbury. http://dx.doi.org/10.5040/9781350970854.055.

Nagel, Alexander, and Christopher S. Wood (2010). *Anachronic Renaissance*. New York: Zone.

Nandy, Ashis (1995). History's Forgotten Doubles. *History and Theory* 34(2): 44–66.

Ndlovu-Gatsheni, Sabelo J. (2018). Rhodes Must Fall. In Sabelo J. Ndlovu-Gatsheni, ed., *Epistemic Freedom in Africa: Deprovincialization and Decolonization*. London: Routledge, 221–242.

Ng, On-cho, and Q. Edward Wang (2005). *Mirroring the Past: The Writing and Use of History in Imperial China*. Honolulu: University of Hawaii Press.

Noble, Safiya Umoja (2018). *Algorithms of Oppression: How Search Engines Reinforce Racism*. New York: New York University Press.

Nordblad, Julia (2021). On the Difference between Anthropocene and Climate Change Temporalities. *Critical Inquiry* 47(2): 328–348.

Nowotny, Helga (1988). From the Future to the Extended Present: Time in Social Systems. In Guy Kirsch, Peter Nijkamp, and Klaus Zimmermann, eds., *The Formulation of Time Preferences in a Multi-disciplinary Perspective: Their Consequences for Individual Behaviour and Collective Decision-Making*. Aldershot: Gower, 17–31.

Nowotny, Helga (1994). *Time: The Modern and Postmodern Experience*. Trans. Neville Plaice. Cambridge: Polity Press.

O'Gorman, Emily, and Andrea Gaynor (2020). More-Than-Human Histories. *Environmental History* 25(4): 711–735.

Olivier, Laurent (1999). The Hochdorf "Princely" Grave and the Question of the Nature of Archaeological Funerary Assemblages. In Tim Murray, ed., *Time and Archaeology*. London: Routledge, 109–138.

Olivier, Laurent (2004). The Past of the Present. Archaeological Memory and Time. *Archaeological Dialogues* 10(2): 204–213.

Olivier, Laurent (2013). Time. In Paul Graves-Brown, Rodney Harrison, and Angela Piccini, eds., *The Oxford Handbook of the Archaeology of the Contemporary World*. Oxford: Oxford University Press, 167–177.

Oppermann, Serpil (2018). The Scale of the Anthropocene. *Mosaic: Interdisciplinary Critical Journal* 51(3): 1–17.

Osborne, Peter (1995). *The Politics of Time: Modernity and Avant-Garde*. London: Verso.

Pereira, Mateus H. F., and Valdei Araujo (2020). Updatism: Gumbrecht's Broad Present, Hartog's Presentism and Beyond. *Diacronie. Studi di Storia Contemporanea* 43(3): 1–20.

Pérez, Moira (2022). Caught between Past and Future: On the Uses of Temporal Figurations for Political Exclusion. In Zoltán Boldizsár Simon and Lars Deile, eds., *Historical Understanding: Past, Present, and Future*. London: Bloomsbury Academic, 35–43.

Pernau, Margrit (2019). Fluid Temporalities: Saiyid Ahmad Khan and the Concept of Modernity. *History and Theory* 57(4): 107–131.

Pernau, Margrit (2021). *Emotions and Temporalities*. Cambridge: Cambridge University Press.

Pettai, Eva-Clarita (2018). Historical Expert Commissions and Their Politics. In Berber Bevernage and Nico Wouters, eds., *The Palgrave Handbook of State-Sponsored History after 1945*. London: Palgrave, 687–712.

Pinder, Wilhelm (1926). *Das Problem der Generation in der Kunstgeschichte*. Berlin: Frankfurter Verlags-Anstalt.

Pomian, Krzysztof (1984). *L'ordre du temps*. Paris: Gallimard.

Ramalho, Walderez (2020). Historical Time between *Chronos* and *Kairos*: On the Historicity of *The Kairos Document* Manifesto, South Africa, 1985. *Rethinking History* 24(3–4): 465–480.

Rampley, Matthew (2022). Linear, Entangled, Anachronic: Periodization and the Shapes of Time in Art History. In Shona Kallestrup, Magdalena Kunińska, Mihnea Alexandru Mihail, Anna Adashinskaya, and Cosmin Minea, eds., *Periodization in the Art Historiographies of Central and Eastern Europe*. New York: Routledge, 14–28.

Rao, Velcheru Narayana, David Shulman, and Sanjay Subrahmanyam (2003). *Textures of Time: Writing History in South India 1600–1800*. New York: Other Press.

Reid, Geneviève, Renée Sieber, and Sammy Blackned (2020). Visions of Time in Geospatial Ontologies from Indigenous Peoples: A Case Study with the Eastern Cree in Northern Quebec. *International Journal of Geographical Information Science* 34(12): 2335–2360.

Retz, Tyson (2022). *Progress and the Scale of History*. Cambridge: Cambridge University Press.

Riofrancos, Thea (2017). *Extractivismo* Unearthed: A Genealogy of a Radical Discourse. *Cultural Studies* 31(2–3): 277–306.

Robin, Libby (2013). Histories for Changing Times: Entering the Anthropocene? *Australian Historical Studies* 44(3): 329–340.

Rockström, Johan, Will Steffen, Kevin Noone et al. (2009). Planetary Boundaries: Exploring the Safe Operating Space for Humanity. *Ecology and Society* 14(2): 32. www.ecologyandsociety.org/vol14/iss2/art32.

Rosa, Hartmut (2013). *Social Acceleration: A New Theory of Modernity*. Trans. Jonathan Trejo-Mathys. New York: Columbia University Press.

Rosa, Hartmut (2020). *The Uncontrollability of the World*. Trans. James C. Wagner. Cambridge: Polity.

Rovelli, Carlo (2018). *The Order of Time*. New York: Riverhead.

Runia, Eelco (2014) *Moved by the Past: Discontinuity and Historical Mutation*. New York: Columbia University Press.

Satia, Priya (2020). *Time's Monster: How History Makes History*. Cambridge, MA: Belknap Press of Harvard University Press.

Sawyer, Stephen W. (2015). Time after Time: Narratives of the Longue Durée in the Anthropocene. *Transatlantica* 1. http://transatlantica.revues.org/7344.

Schiffman, Zachary Sayre (2011). *The Birth of the Past*. Baltimore, MD: Johns Hopkins University Press.

Schwartz, Frederic J. (2001). Ernst Bloch and Wilhelm Pinder: Out of Sync. *Grey Room* 3: 54–89.

Serres, Michel, with Bruno Latour (1995). *Conversations on Science, Culture, and Time*. Trans. Roxanne Lapidus. Ann Arbor: University of Michigan Press.

Simmel, Georg (2002). The Metropolis and Mental Life. In Gary Bridge and Sophie Watson, eds., *The Blackwell City Reader*. Oxford: Wiley-Blackwell, 11–19.

Simon, Zoltán Boldizsár (2019a). *History in Times of Unprecedented Change: A Theory for the 21st Century*. London: Bloomsbury Academic.

Simon, Zoltán Boldizsár (2019b). The Transformation of Historical Time: Processual and Evental Temporalities. In Marek Tamm and Laurent Olivier, eds., *Rethinking Historical Time: New Approaches to Presentism*. London: Bloomsbury Academic, 71–84.

Simon, Zoltán Boldizsár (2019c). The Story of Humanity and the Challenge of Posthumanity. *History of the Human Sciences* 32(2): 101–120.

Simon, Zoltán Boldizsár (2019d). Two Cultures of the Posthuman Future. *History and Theory* 58(2): 171–184.

Simon, Zoltán Boldizsár (2020). *The Epochal Event: Transformations in the Human, Technological, and Natural Worlds*. Cham: Palgrave.

Simon, Zoltán Boldizsár (2021). Domesticating the Future through History. *Time and Society* 30(4): 494–516.

Simon, Zoltán Boldizsár, and Marek Tamm (2021). Historical Futures. *History and Theory* 60(1): 3–22.

Smocovitis, V. B. (1992). Unifying Biology: The Evolutionary Synthesis and Evolutionary Biology. *Journal of the History of Biology* 25(1): 1–65.

Sörlin, Sverker (2022). Environmental Times: Synchronizing Human-Earth Temporalities from *Annales* to Anthropocene, 1920s–2020s. In Anders Ekström and Staffan Bergwik, eds., *Times of History, Times of Nature: Temporalization and the Limits of Modern Knowledge*. New York: Berghahn, 64–101.

Sörlin, Sverker, and Erik Isberg (2021). Synchronizing Earthly Timescales: Ice, Pollen, and the Making of Proto-Anthropocene Knowledge in the North Atlantic Region. *Annals of the American Association of Geographers* 111 (3): 717–728.

Sorokin, Pitirim A., and Robert K. Merton (1937). Social Time: A Methodological and Functional Analysis. *American Journal of Sociology* 42(5): 615–629.

Sousa Santos, Boaventura de (2009). A Non-Occidentalist West? Learned Ignorance and Ecology of Knowledge. *Theory, Culture & Society* 26(7–8): 103–125.

Steffen, Will, Wendy Broadgate, Lisa Deutsch, Owen Gaffney, and Cornelia Ludwig. (2015a). The Trajectory of the Anthropocene: The Great Acceleration. *Anthropocene Review* 2(1): 81–98.

Steffen, Will, Katherine Richardson, Johan Rockström et al. (2015b). Planetary Boundaries: Guiding Human Development on a Changing Planet. *Science* 347(6223): 1259855.

Steffen, Will, Reinhold Leinfelder, Jan Zalasiewicz et al. (2016). Stratigraphic and Earth System Approaches to Defining the Anthropocene. *Earth's Future* 4: 324–345.

Steffen, Will, Katherine Richardson, Johan Rockström et al. (2020). The Emergence and Evolution of Earth System Science. *Nature Reviews Earth & Environment* 1: 54–63.

Steinmetz, Willibald, Zoltán Boldizsár Simon, and Kirill Postoutenko (2021). Temporal Comparisons: Evaluating the World through Historical Time. *Time & Society* 30(4): 447–461.

Swenson, Edward, and Andrew P. Roddick (2018). Introduction: Rethinking Temporality and Historicity from the Perspective of Andean Archaeology.

In Edward Swenson and Andrew Roddick, eds., *Constructions of Time and History in the Pre-Columbian Andes*. Boulder: University Press of Colorado, 3–43.

Taillandier, Apolline (2021). "Staring into the Singularity" and Other Posthuman Tales: Transhumanist Stories of Future Change. *History and Theory* 60(2): 215–233.

Táíwò, Olúfẹ́mi O. (2022). *Reconsidering Reparations*. Oxford: Oxford University Press.

Tamm, Marek (2015). Introduction: Afterlife of Events: Perspectives on Mnemohistory. In Marek Tamm, ed., *Afterlife of Events: Perspectives on Mnemohistory*. Basingstoke: Palgrave Macmillan, 1–23.

Tamm, Marek (2019). Introduction: Juri Lotman's Semiotic Theory of History and Cultural Memory. In Marek Tamm, ed., *Juri Lotman. Culture, Memory and History: Essays in Cultural Semiotics*. Cham: Palgrave Macmillan, 1–26.

Tamm, Marek (2022a). Future-Oriented History. In Zoltán Boldizsár Simon and Lars Deile, eds., *Historical Understanding: Past, Present, and Future*. London: Bloomsbury Academic, 131–140.

Tamm, Marek (2022b). Lotman and Cultural History. In Marek Tamm and Peeter Torop, eds., *The Companion to Juri Lotman: A Semiotic Theory of Culture*. London: Bloomsbury Academic, 334–349.

Tamm, Marek, and Laurent Olivier (2019). Introduction: Rethinking Historical Time. In Marek Tamm and Laurent Olivier, eds., *Rethinking Historical Time: New Approaches to Presentism*. London: Bloomsbury Academic, 1–20.

Tamm, Marek, and Zoltán Boldizsár Simon (2020). Historical Thinking and the Human: Introduction. *Journal of the Philosophy of History* 14(3): 285–309.

Tanaka, Stefan (2019). *History without Chronology*. Amherst, MA: Lever Press.

Thomas, Julia Adeney (2014). History and Biology in the Anthropocene: Problems of Scale, Problems of Value. *American Historical Review* 119(5): 1587–1607.

Thomas, Julia Adeney (2019). Why the "Anthropocene" Is Not "Climate Change" and Why It Matters. *Asia Global Online*, January 10. www .asiaglobalonline.hku.hk/anthropocene-climate-change.

Thomas, Julia Adeney, ed. (2022). *Altered Earth: Getting the Anthropocene Right*. Cambridge: Cambridge University Press.

Thomas, Peter D. (2017). The Plural Temporalities of Hegemony. *Rethinking Marxism* 29(2): 281–302.

Tomba, Massimiliano (2013). *Marx's Temporalities*. Trans. Peter D. Thomas and Sara R. Farris. Leiden: Brill.

Torpey, John (2003). Introduction: Politics and the Past. In John Torpey, ed., *Politics and the Past: On Repairing Historical Injustices*. Lanham, MD: Rowman & Littlefield, 1–34.

Torres, Felipe (2022). *Temporal Regimes: Materiality, Politics, Technology*. London: Routledge.

Urry, John (2000). *Sociology beyond Societies: Mobilities for the Twenty-First Century*. London: Routledge.

Veland, Siri, and Amanda H. Lynch (2016). Scaling the Anthropocene: How the Stories We Tell Matter. *Geoforum* 72: 1–5.

Vinge, Vernor (1993). The Coming Technological Singularity: How to Survive in the Post-human Era. In *Vision-21: Interdisciplinary Science and Engineering in the Era of Cyberspace*. Proceedings of a Symposium Cosponsored by the NASA Lewis Research Center and the Ohio Aerospace Institute, Westlake, Ohio, March 30–31, 1993, 11–22. https://ntrs.nasa.gov/citations/19940022856.

Virilio, Paul (1986). *Speed and Politics: An Essay on Dromology*. Trans. Mark Polizzotti. New York: Semiotext(e).

Virilio, Paul (2010). *The Futurism of the Instant: Stop-Eject*. Trans. Julie Rose. Cambridge: Polity.

Virilio, Paul (2012). *The Great Accelerator*. Trans. Julie Rose. Cambridge: Polity.

Wajcman, Judy (2015). *Pressed for Time: The Acceleration of Life in Digital Capitalism*. Chicago, IL: University of Chicago Press.

Welch, Cheryl B. (2003). Colonial Violence and the Rhetoric of Evasion: Tocqueville on Algeria. *Political Theory* 31(2): 235–264.

West-Pavlov, Russell (2013). *Temporalities*. London: Routledge.

Whyte, Kyle (2017). Indigenous Climate Change Studies: Indigenizing Futures, Decolonizing the Anthropocene. *English Language Notes* 55(1–2): 153–162.

Wiggin, Bethany, Carolyn Fornoff, and Patricia Eunji Kim (2020). Introduction: Environmental Humanities across Times, Disciplines, and Research Practices. In Bethany Wiggin, Carolyn Fornoff, and Patricia Eunji Kim, eds., *Timescales: Thinking across Ecological Temporalities*. Minneapolis: University of Minnesota Press, vii–xxviii.

Witmore, Christopher (2006). Vision, Media, Noise and the Percolation of Time. *Journal of Material Culture* 11(3): 267–292.

Woolf, Daniel (2021). Getting Back to Normal: On Normativity in History and Historiography. *History and Theory* 60(3): 469–512.

Zalasiewicz, Jan, Colin N. Waters, Erle C. Ellis, Martin J. Head, Davor Vidas, Will Steffen et al. (2021). The Anthropocene: Comparing Its Meaning in Geology (Chronostratigraphy) with Conceptual Approaches Arising in Other Disciplines. *Earth's Future* 9(3): 1–25.

Acknowledgments

We are grateful to Chris Lorenz and Daniel Woolf for their useful comments on the first version of the manuscript. Marek Tamm's research was supported by Estonian Research Council grant PRG1276.

Cambridge Elements ☰

Historical Theory and Practice

Daniel Woolf
Queen's University, Ontario

Daniel Woolf is Professor of History at Queen's University, Ontario, where he served
for ten years as principal and vice-chancellor, and has held academic appointments at
a number of Canadian universities. He is the author or editor of several books and articles on
the history of historical thought and writing, and on early modern British intellectual history,
including most recently *A Concise History of History* (Cambridge University Press 2019).
He is a fellow of the Royal Historical Society, the Royal Society of Canada, and the Society of
Antiquaries of London. He is married with three adult children.

About the Series
Cambridge Elements in Historical Theory and Practice is a series intended for a wide range
of students, scholars, and others whose interests involve engagement with the past.
Topics include the theoretical, ethical, and philosophical issues involved in doing history,
the interconnections between history and other disciplines and questions of method,
and the application of historical knowledge to contemporary global and social issues
such as climate change, reconciliation and justice, heritage, and identity politics.

Cambridge Elements $\equiv$

Historical Theory and Practice

Elements in the Series

The Theory and Philosophy of History: Global Variations
João Ohara

A History of Political Science
Mark Bevir

The Transformation of History in the Digital Age
Ian Milligan

Historians' Virtues: From Antiquity to the Twenty-First Century
Herman Paul

Confronting Evil in History
Daniel Little

Progress and the Scale of History
Tyson Retz

Collaborative Historical Research in the Age of Big Data: Lessons from an Interdisciplinary Project
Ruth Ahnert, Emma In, Mia Ridge and Giorgia Tolfo

A History of Big History
Ian Hesketh

The Fabric of Historical Time
Zoltán Boldizsár Simon and Marek Tamm

A full series listing is available at: www.cambridge.org/EHTP